The Daily Disciplines of Leadership

Douglas B. Reeves

The Daily Disciplines of Leadership

How to Improve Student Achievement,
Staff Motivation, and
Personal Organization

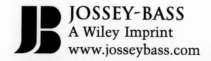

JOSSEY-BASS
A Wiley Imprint
www.josseybass.com

Published by Jossey-Bass
A Wiley Imprint
989 Market Street, San Francisco, CA 94103-1741   www.josseybass.com

Jossey-Bass books and products are available through most bookstores. To contact Jossey-Bass directly call our Customer Care Department within the U.S. at 800-956-7739, outside the U.S. at 317-572-3986, or fax 317-572-4002.

Jossey-Bass also publishes its books in a variety of electronic formats. Some content that appears in print may not be available in electronic books.

Library of Congress Cataloging-in-Publication Data

Reeves, Douglas B., 1953–
    The daily disciplines of leadership : how to improve student
achievement, staff motivation, and personal organization / Douglas B.
Reeves. — 1st ed.
        p.   cm. — (The Jossey-Bass education series)
    Includes bibliographical references (p. 225) and index.
    ISBN-13 978-0-7879-6403-0 (alk. paper)
    ISBN-10 0-7879-6403-4 (alk. paper)
    ISBN-13 978-0-7879-8767-1 (paperback)
    ISBN-10 0-7879-8767-0 (paperback)
    1. Educational leadership. 2. School management and organization. 3.
School improvement programs. I. Title. II. Series.
    LB2806 .R365   2002
    371.2—dc21   2002011848

Printed in the United States of America
FIRST EDITION
HB Printing   10 9 8 7 6 5 4 3 2 1
PB Printing   10 9 8 7 6 5 4 3 2

The Jossey-Bass Education Series

To General Stephen Reeves, whose country is lucky to have him in a time of need, and whose family bursts with pride

Contents

List of Tables, Figures, and Exhibits

Preface

Since publication of the first edition of *The Daily Disciplines of Leadership* in 2002, the educational, economic, and political landscape in the United States and throughout the world has changed in a dramatic fashion. Within the United States, federal and state requirements have elevated educational accountability to historically high levels. Throughout the world, the globalization of industry, capital, and labor has had profound effects on teachers and school leaders in nearly every nation. Despite a downturn in the technology sector of the economy in the late 1990s and the shock of terrorist attacks in 2001, U.S. economic growth and the consequent demand for educated workers have continued at a pace that is unmatched since the end of World War II. Growth in this country, however, pales in comparison to the double-digit growth in Asian economies, with parts of China completing a decade of growth exceeding 20 percent per year. While U.S. educational standards were increasing to an unparalleled degree in the past ten years, China increased the number of key universities by a factor of twelve over the same period of time. Throughout the developed and developing world, however, one factor has remained constant: the need for effective educational leadership is greater than ever.

During the same number of years, I have traveled more than two million miles, visiting schools and observing educational leaders in all fifty states and five continents. The essential messages of *Daily Disciplines* remain relevant today and are reinforced by large-scale research and numerous case studies that my colleagues and I have completed in the past several years. In particular, there are six big ideas in the following pages that are more important now than ever.

First, *leadership and management are inseparable*. Effective leadership requires an essential set of skills, including management of time, projects, and people. Although it remains in vogue to elevate "leadership" over "management" (check the frequency of use of those two terms in graduate school courses, professional development catalogues, and book titles), the dichotomy between leadership and management has been counterproductive. Vision, mission, and strategy—the mantras of many leadership courses— are fine things, but they are impotent without fundamental management skills. Neither advanced technology nor the latest leadership insights will liberate us from the limits of time, the need for organization, or the imperatives of human relationships.

Second, *accountability is more than test scores*. The Leadership and Learning Matrix, first published in this book, has become the foundation for an exceptional amount of research and practice linking student performance with the "antecedents of excellence"—measurable practices in teaching and leadership. Far from an esoteric theory, the matrix has helped school systems throughout the world communicate about accountability in an entirely new way. Rather than using a single set of test scores to represent students' results, schools can hold adults as accountable as students.

Third, *leadership leverage* is the key to maximizing results in an era of higher expectations and limited resources. The best example of leadership leverage I have found so far is the relationship between nonfiction writing and improved results in every subject. When students learn to describe, persuade, and analyze using the written word, their performance improves in every other academic area. When educators diminish their emphasis on writing because their local testing authorities have abandoned the testing of this vital skill, they make a terrible trade-off, saving a little money and time with the sacrifice of lifelong multidisciplinary skills that students need.

Fourth, *feedback is as important for adults as it is for students*. The most disengaged and inattentive student will happily wile away hours in pursuit of the next level of an electronic game. Why? I'm a good teacher, but I am forced to wonder what Nintendo provides that I have failed to provide in my math and writing classes. Nintendo and its many imitators provide feedback—and not just the feedback of my feeble report card. Nintendo provides feedback that is immediate, accurate, specific, and incremental. Kids who play

Nintendo do not ask, "How can I become a grand master?" but rather, "How can I get to the next level?" So it must be with leaders. Our pursuit of mythical perfection—the leader as Attila the Hun, Elizabeth I, Franklin Roosevelt, or a host of other idols—is unwise and unproductive. While too many graduate schools of educational leadership seek to produce the next FDR (and more than a few produce the next Attila), the question on the lips of most education leaders with whom I confer on a daily basis is this: "How can I be a more effective leader *tomorrow?*" Teachers ask the same question. They do not aspire to be Socrates or Jamie Escalante. They simply want to have one or two ideas that they can implement *tomorrow.*

Fifth, *students are not customers*. After writing more than twenty books and many articles in the professional and popular press, I have been pleasantly surprised that the few paragraphs in *Daily Disciplines* which argue that students are not customers are the most frequently quoted and reproduced lines I have ever written. Despite our consumerist society, the essential truth is that customers receive instant gratification, whereas students continue to thank us years—even decades—after the fact. Shelley Sackett is our local school board president, mother to three public school kids, and, last of all, my wife. I've watched as high school graduates accept a diploma from her hands, throw their hats into the air, and run out of the stadium, graduation gowns flowing in the wind—and very few of them stop to thank the teachers and school leaders who helped them through the previous thirteen years. Customers expect to receive satisfaction instantly and express their gratitude upon the completion of a transaction. The interactions between students and teachers, in contrast, are not short-term transactions, but a complex set of interactions with lifelong impact.

Sixth, the *value of strategic planning lies not in nicely formatted documents, but in a focus on core values, clear strategies, and effective action plans*. Research that my colleagues at the Center for Performance Assessment and I have conducted suggested that format perfection is inversely related to student achievement. Thus *Daily Disciplines* got it precisely right when it suggested that we "save strategic planning from strategic plans." Although planning is a necessary discipline for every leader, the best plans are brief, focused, and clear. The best plans are distinguished not by jargon and complexity, but by their relevance to the daily lives of students, teachers, and leaders.

In the following pages, you may not find mystical inspiration or earth-shattering insights, but I promise that you will find practical ideas that you can use *tomorrow*. The life of a writer is one of regret—the only thing worse than missing a deadline is meeting the deadline and then thinking of all the things that could have been written. *Daily Disciplines* remains a work in progress, as I continue to listen to educational leaders throughout the world and improve my understanding of the relationship between leadership and student achievement.

Before the end of the first decade of the twenty-first century, almost half of current school leaders will retire or leave the profession. New leaders will be confronted with a bewildering array of challenges, not the least of which is the tendency of school systems to give the newest and least experienced leaders the most challenging schools with the least experienced faculties. Every leader must ultimately confront the fact that there are two theoretical in-boxes on the desk. The first in-box is huge, overflowing, and bottomless; it bears the label "Things I Cannot Control." The second, much smaller in-box is the heart of effective leadership. This in-box, labeled "Things I Can Influence," is where effective leaders invest their time, energy, and emotion. For decades, giants in the field of educational leadership research, such as John Goodlad, have reminded us of the fundamental truth that effective leadership has a positive impact on student achievement, educational equity, staff morale, and organizational effectiveness. Leaders who are consumed by the first in-box rarely have the opportunity to get to the second one. My wish for you is that you acknowledge the first in-box but not be consumed by it. Invest your energy in the leadership strategies, such as those you will learn in the following pages, that have the greatest impact on student achievement. When you return home exhausted after another challenging day, you will have the satisfaction of knowing that another day of your professional life has been invested wisely and that you have made a profound difference for children and for the world.

Acknowledgments

One would think that after a fourteenth book my list of acknowledgements would grow shorter. With each new writing project, I realize that the list is endless, and I am embarrassed that I have recognized decades of scholarship of others with a mere footnote. The words that appear here—footnotes to footnotes—attempt to say what book titles and interview titles in a reference list fail to express. Anne Bryant, executive director of the National School Boards Association, is generous with her time and passionate in her commitment to public education. Her organization and its publications set the standard for practical ideas, rigorous research, and civil discourse. Paul Houston is more than the executive director of the American Association of School Administrators; he is one of the leading public advocates for the truth about public education and its teachers and leaders. He is also the architect of some of the most important links between thinking, strategy, and action in the last decade. Dennis Sparks has, with a small and brilliant team, transformed staff development from the stepchild of the central office to a driving force in educational reform. His efforts put the maxim "knowledge is power" into action on behalf of the nation's schoolchildren.

"Those who can," the adage goes, "do." To which I would add, "Those can do more, teach and lead in today's challenging educational environment." Some of the teachers, leaders, and thinkers who have influenced this particular volume are Lucy McCormick Calkins, Linda Darling-Hammond, David Driscoll, Richard Elmore, Chester Finn Jr., Tom Guskey, Bill Habermehl, Kati

Haycock, Jeff Howard, Tom Kite, Audrey Kleinsasser, Thom Lockamy, Robert Marzano, Betty McNally, Alan Moore, Rod Paige, Kathy Peckron, Dennis Peterson, Milli Pierce, Richard Rothstein, Stan Scheer, Mike Schmoker, Ray Simon, Rick Stiggins, Don Thompson, Terry Thompson, Grant Wiggins, Chris Wright, and Karen Young.

My colleagues at the Center for Performance Assessment are a continuing source of challenge and wisdom. Larry Ainsworth, Eileen Allison, Chris Benavides, Nan Caldwell, Cheryl Dunkle, Anne Fenske, Tony Flach, Bette Frazier, Paul Kane, Michele LePatner, Jill Lewis, Janelle Miller, Craig Ross, Stacy Scott, Devon Sheldon, Mike White, Nan Woodson, and their colleagues at the center offer their careers as testimony to their single-minded commitment to the principle that leadership and learning are inextricably linked. My thanks also go to Esmond Harmsworth, of the Zachary Shuster Harmsworth Literary Agency, and to Lesley Iura, Pamela Berkman, and Tom Finnegan of Jossey-Bass. Tom's meticulous editing and thoughtful challenges helped bring clarity to what is frequently a complex and opaque subject.

My thinking was inevitably shaped by a heritage of leaders and learners, including a grandmother, Laura Anderson Johnson, who served as a school superintendent in the early days of the twentieth century; and my father, Jean Brooks Reeves, who served as a combat leader in the Second World War and was surely as much a teacher then as he was in his last days as a professor. Among his final gifts to his children and grandchildren was a redefinition of lifelong learning and the vision of a dying man listening to unabridged books on Greek history. Living and learning, he taught us, are inextricably linked.

The nation needs military leaders who know the value of education as well. One of those leaders is my brother, U.S. Army General Stephen Reeves. My other brother, Andrew, is a volunteer coach who shares his time and resources with children, who relish his thoughtful balance of enthusiasm and fair play.

Closer to home, my wife, Shelley Sackett, recently won a narrow victory in a race for our local school board, an endeavor that some describe as lunacy but that makes me burst with pride. She gives our children a model of how we owe our energies not only to ourselves and our families but to the entire community. Words like *strategy* and *discipline* can seem barren and devoid of passion. Brooks, Julia, Alex, and James are my daily reminder that behind the strategies of educational leadership there must be a burning intensity that can only be sustained by an abiding love of children.

Douglas B. Reeves
Swampscott, Massachusetts
August 2002

The Author

Douglas B. Reeves—one of the nation's leading authorities on academic standards, performance assessment, and accountability—is chairman and founder of the Center for Performance Assessment. He is the author of more than twenty books, including *The Leader's Guide to Standards* (Jossey-Bass, 2002). Reeves was twice named to the Distinguished Authors Series by the Harvard University Graduate School of Education and won the Parent's Choice Award for his book, *20-Minute Learning Connection*. He was also named a Brock International Laureate, one of the most significant education awards in the world.

Books for Parents, Educators, and School Leaders by Douglas Reeves

101 Questions and Answers About Standards, Assessment, and Accountability (Denver: Advanced Learning Press, 2000)

20-Minute Learning Connection: A Practical Guide for Parents Who Want to Help Their Children Succeed in School (New York: Simon & Schuster, 2001)

Accountability in Action: A Blueprint for Learning Organizations (Denver: Advanced Learning Press, 2000)

Crusade in the Classroom: How George W. Bush's Education Reforms Will Affect Your Children, Our Schools (New York: Simon & Schuster, 2001)

The Leader's Guide to Standards (San Francisco: Jossey-Bass, 2002)

Holistic Accountability: Serving Students, Schools, and Community (Thousand Oaks, Calif.: Corwin, 2002)

Making Standards Work: How to Implement Standards-Based Performance Assessments in the Classroom, School, and District (3rd edition) (Denver: Advanced Learning Press, 2002)

Reason to Write: Help Your Child Succeed in School and in Life Through Deeper Thinking, Better Reasoning, and Clearer Communication (New York: Simon & Schuster, 2002)

The Reason to Write Student Workbook (New York: Simon & Schuster, 2002)

The Daily Disciplines of Leadership

Part One

Leadership Essentials

Chapter One

Students Are Not Customers

The Unique Elements of Educational Leadership

Leadership Keys

Students are not customers

Leaders are architects of improved performance

Results are not enough

Leaders understand the antecedents of excellence

Equity is not optional

Values and principles: a harbor during the inevitable storm

Leadership is an intimidating subject and an even more challenging role. There are more than twenty-six thousand books in print that claim to be about this subject; thus if description and instruction were sufficient, one would think that the world is filled with successful leaders. Nevertheless, when I ask people to name as many truly successful leaders as they can—those they know and those they have only become acquainted with through newspapers and history books—the tally is rarely more than one or two dozen. When I further challenge them to identify whether the leader was merely at the right place at the right time—the lucky leader, as we shall call them in this volume—the list is cut by more than half.

This leads me to bad news, worse news, and good news. The bad news is clear: excellent leadership is rare. The worse news is that you do not become an excellent leader by reading this or any other book. We authors hate admitting that our books do not cure wrinkles, induce weight loss, and ignite the hidden qualities that had, before a trip to the bookstore, been dormant.

This brings us to the less obvious good news: excellent leadership is an acquired skill. It is not a talent endowed at birth. It is not a character trait developed in childhood by parents. It is not a matter of luck, at least if we define *leader* appropriately as the architect of sustained improvement of individual and organizational performance.

Students Are Not Customers

The Enduring Impact of an Educational Leader

"I never told you this before, but you helped me to stop being afraid of school, and that changed my life."

I did not recognize the tall young man near the bargain table of the Tattered Cover bookstore, my favorite hangout during the time I lived in the Rocky Mountains. He then extended his hand and explained, "I'm Marcus, and you were my teacher in sixth grade."

Ah, yes—Marcus. He was the smallest kid in the class, and as often as not recess ended in tears. The transition from playground to the classroom was not much better, where many of the other kids needed him for his ability to translate their questions into English but appeared not to return the favor when Marcus needed help. Every exercise was a struggle and every mistake was a terror that reminded him of his inadequacies. If there had been any doubt, his peers (and apparently his parents) reinforced his self-doubt. Marcus responded to encouragement and small victories, routinely staying after class or coming in early to ensure that he had not only solved a problem but understood it.

As the year went on, the students took more responsibility for blackboard work; I learned that daily demonstrations that I knew the Pythagorean Theorem were less meaningful than those moments when my students assumed the role of teacher and demonstrated their own understanding. This was hardly a risk-free endeavor, as student mistakes were accompanied by catcalls from peers. Skeptical administrators wondered aloud about who the teacher was when they observed children, rather than the appointed expert, holding the chalk and addressing the class. More than once, Marcus had stumbled and retreated to his desk in tears. Perhaps a kinder teacher would have relieved him of the obligation to present a lesson, but I knew that my task was a difficult balance between gentle encouragement and uncompromising demands.

The day that Marcus presented in clear and precise language, using numbers, symbols, and words, that the square of the hypotenuse was equal to the sum of the square of the two sides of a right triangle, he did not know that the principal, Mr. Robinson, and his mother were outside the door listening. A moment after his successful presentation of the proof, the eavesdroppers entered the room. Mrs. Bencista was beaming. Mr. Robinson added in his typical businesslike fashion, "That was excellent." Marcus said nothing, but from that day forward, his confidence and demeanor changed.

In our brief encounter in the bookstore, Marcus explained that he had become a successful diamond merchant, a business in which visual acuity was second only to business acumen. "I use what you taught me every day," he said. "Thank you." Perhaps Marcus meant that he used mathematics, but I suspect that he also benefits from the resilience, perseverance, and tenacity that I attempted to instill in all of my students. I am fairly certain, however, that the thanks Marcus offered would not have been merited if I had created a classroom characterized by false reassurance and the absence of challenge.

Delayed Gratification: The Essential Difference Between Students and Customers

If you have been an educator for several years, perhaps you have enjoyed the experience of a student thanking you for something that you did five, ten, or fifteen years ago. The unexpected and satisfying encounter typically occurs when a former student is only now recognizing the importance of our insistence on quality, perseverance, and risk taking. Veteran educators know that if we curried favor with our students through low expectation, profligate reward, and scant challenge in the classroom, the transient appreciation from students would soon be replaced by contempt. We knew from our own experience that we never thanked our least demanding teachers during chance encounters at a bookstore. Of course, the appreciation of students that is fifteen years after an event does not appear on a teacher evaluation. Most leaders live in the present, with today's complaints and tomorrow's praise. Rather than inquire into the long-term consequences of a strategy, the educational leader is much more likely to ask, "What have you done for me lately?"

Adopting the vernacular of the business world, we wonder if the customers are satisfied. Our focus is on the short-term; in other words, it not only obscures consideration of the long-term but can be a perverse incentive at cross-purposes. A customer needs instant gratification; a student needs challenge. A customer needs to be happy; a student needs to be provoked into deliberate dissatisfaction, reflection, and hard work before the genuine happiness of discovery and learning can take place. Customers can take revenge on a merchant by withholding their money. Students take revenge on themselves by withholding participation, withdrawing from learning, proving with their failure the accuracy of their appraisal of the teacher as incompetent.

There is one more distinction worthy of mention. The merchant can advertise, develop new products and, she hopes, find new customers. Educators and school leaders, by contrast, must face the same students tomorrow, including those who are unhappy, dissatisfied, bored, unmotivated, nonparticipative, and without a strong support system at home.

Educational leaders who view students as customers accept a world of superficiality, mediocrity, instant gratification, and, as a result, popularity. Educational leaders who reject this view risk their short-term popularity but remain true to their values. They replace superficiality with depth, mediocrity with excellence, and instant gratification with appreciation years in the future. Some of the techniques in this book yield improved student results with astonishing speed, but other strategies require commitment to the unending enterprise of learning. The leader who pursues this path does not ride into the sunset with a mission definitively accomplished but instead continues each day to make a difference in the lives of the students, teachers, parents, and communities served. This book does not help you make it as if there were a clear destination; rather, it assists you on an unending journey of leadership excellence.

What Business and Educational Leaders Can Learn from One Another

The contention that students are not customers is not a declaration that business and educational leaders have nothing to learn from one another. In fact, many innovations from business have been useful in education. Just as the best business leaders know that the proverbial bottom line does not tell the complete story of business performance, the best educational leaders know that accountability is more than a litany of test scores (Kaplan and Norton, 2001; Epstein and Birchard, 1999). Consider the case of Warren Buffet, frequently regarded as the world's shrewdest investor. Although his status in business circles as "the sage of Omaha" appeared secure in the early 1990s and is certainly so today, there was an interval when investors had their doubts. Because he followed the rule that "I don't invest in things that I don't understand," Buffet failed to follow legions of other investors into the Internet boom of the late 1990s. When small companies without substantial assets and with multimillion dollar losses nevertheless became stock market darlings, Buffet refused to follow the fad. The stock market performance of his company, Berkshire Hathaway, was stellar when viewed with the perspective of decades, but the stock lagged significantly behind the typical dot-com miracle company that appeared to enrich investors overnight with triple-digit gains.

Thus to his critics, the sage of Omaha became just another has-
been who clearly didn't get it. There were, for the first time ever,
scattered boos at the 1999 annual meeting of shareholders of
Berkshire Hathaway, presumably from investors disgruntled that
Buffet heeded his rule to avoid investing where it did not, to him
at least, make sense. A year later, when the twenty-something
paper billionaires were hocking their BMWs, layoffs and bank-
ruptcies were a common event, and the bloom was off the dot-com
rose, Buffet's wisdom was evident. He understood that a focus on
short-term results was an appealing but dangerous trap. Most
important, he saw that blind association of success with a rising
stock price represented a fundamental analytical failure to associate real causes with real effects.

This is a lesson the successful educational leader has long
known: results are not enough. Unless the leader understands the
causes associated with improved educational achievement, she
cannot make informed decisions in the future. Just as Buffet
endured the boos of disgruntled shareholders, the successful educational leader must accept some unpopularity as she challenges
time-honored tradition, insists on data to support prejudice, and
makes difficult decisions. A successful leader in any context, however, understands the fundamental importance of causal analysis
and thus does not chase every fad simply because it was in the
temporal or physical vicinity of apparent results.

In business, this complexity is recognized through use of the
"balanced scorecard" (Kaplan and Norton, 1996). As the dot-com
boom and bust instructed us, neither rising stock prices nor transient enthusiasm is sufficient to maintain an enterprise. In education, applying holistic accountability (Reeves, 2002b) systems
allows similar understanding. It is not test scores alone that tell the
story of a successful classroom or school, but rather deeper understanding of the antecedents of excellence that reveals the factors
associated with student achievement. The problem with this
approach to leadership is that it elevates analysis of root causes over
superficial presentation of today's effects. This dilemma is at the

heart of what makes educational leadership unique: students are not customers.

The Purpose of Leadership

Take a pencil—not a pen—and write in the space below your response to this question: What is the purpose of educational leadership?

When I pose this question to leaders without imposing a border the size of a business card, I typically receive an answer that is (to be charitable) ponderous, unfocused, and unrelated to the daily activities of the leader who offered the explanation. Typically, the training for such an unproductive exercise in loquaciousness was a strategic planning process that culminated in a page-long mission statement, a plan with hundreds of objectives, and administrators who were able to walk authoritatively down the hallway, reeking of leather as they carried THE PLAN with them.

Here are definitions of effective leadership from some of the world's leading experts on the subject:

> Those who help us center our work in a deeper purpose are leaders we cherish, and to whom we return love, gift for gift [Wheatley, 1999, p. 133].

I'm talking about *leadership* as the development of vision and strategies, the alignment of relevant people behind those strategies, and the empowerment of individuals to make the vision happen, despite obstacles. This stands in stark contrast with *management,* which involves keeping the current system operating through planning, budgeting, organizing, staffing, controlling, and problem-solving. Leadership works through people and culture. It's soft and hot. Management works through hierarchy and systems. It's harder and cooler [Kotter, 1999, p. 10; emphasis in original].

Leaders manage the dream. All leaders have the capacity to create a compelling vision, one that takes people to a new place, and the ability to translate that vision into reality [Bennis, 1999, p. 26].

Leaders produce consent, others seek consensus. Consent is given to the confident and composed, those with firm and persuasive convictions. Only people who believe in themselves generate believers. Nor is it a matter of charisma. It is about inner strength and clearly articulated views that are convincingly based on deep experience and solid judgments. Arrogance and swagger sometimes work, but then things fall apart [Levitt, 1991, p. 30].

We believe that, above all else, strategic leaders must have a sense of vision [similar to Christopher Columbus]—an ability to set broad, lofty goals and steer a course toward them, but with the insight and flexibility to adjust both the course and the goals as the horizon becomes clearer. They must be able to communicate the goals and the course to well-educated, technically skilled colleagues. And they must develop the internal and external alliances and supporting communication and reward structures that will ensure the appropriate resources are brought to bear on achieving the organization's strategic objective [Vicere and Fulmer, 1997, pp. 2–3].

The function of leadership is to cope with change. Leadership did not have any real meaning in the marketplace until recently, when radical change became the norm. . . . To lead change, skills are needed for creating an attractive vision of the future and making it a real possibility. The test of good leadership is the achievement of intended change in systems and people [Shtogren, 1999, pp. 2–3].

Most management writers agree that leadership is *the process of influencing the activities of an individual or a group in efforts toward goal achievement in a given situation.* From this definition of leadership, it follows that the leadership process is a function of the *leader,* the *follower,* and other *situational* variables—L = $f(l, f, s)$ [Hersey and Blanchard, 1993, p. 93; italics in original].

Leaders in learning organizations . . . focus predominantly on purpose and systemic structure. Moreover, they "teach" people through the organization to do likewise [Senge, 1990, p. 353].

The builders of visionary companies tend to be clock builders, not time tellers. They concentrate primarily on building an organization—building a ticking clock—rather than on hitting a market just right with a visionary product idea and riding the growth curve of an attractive product life cycle. And instead of concentrating on acquiring the individual personality traits of visionary leadership, they take an architectural approach and concentrate on building the organizational traits of visionary companies. The primary output of their efforts is not the tangible implementation of a great idea, the expression of a charismatic personality, the gratification of their ego, or the accumulation of personal wealth. Their greatest creation is *the company itself* and what it stands for [Collins and Porras, 1994, p. 23; emphasis in original].

Management exists for the sake of the institution's results. It has to start with the intended results and has to organize the resources of the institution to attain these results. It is the organ to make the institution, whether business, church, university, hospital or a battered women's shelter, capable of producing results outside of itself [Drucker, 1999, p. 39].

My addition to this list: *leaders are the architects of improved individual and organizational performance*.

The Implications of the Leader as Architect

My ten-word definition has several important implications. First, the architect designs, but does not do, the work of building. Without welders, carpenters, electricians, bricklayers, engineers, surveyors, painters, and host of other specialists, the architect is merely a dreamer with drawings. In this context, we know not only what the leader does but what the leader does not do—indeed, cannot do. The leader cannot be simultaneously an expert in writing, calculus, school finance, physics, assessment, personnel management, European history, chemistry, parent engagement, child development, classroom management, student motivation, and the host of other expectations that we routinely expect of the educational leader.

Second, the successful leader is, by definition, dissatisfied with the status quo. Because the emphasis is on improvement at the individual and organizational levels, the sentiment that "everything is just fine, so please leave us alone" is alien to this leader. Dissatisfaction with the present does not imply discontent. Indeed, the effective leader appears to be addicted to celebration, whether it is the first sentence attempted by a kindergartner, the first experiment with alternative schedules by a fourth grade teacher, or the twenty-eighth year of new learning by a veteran physical education teacher. The context of the celebration, however, is never "Now we can stop working" but rather "I can't wait to see what you're going to do next!"

The third and most important implication of my definition of leadership is the inclusive emphasis on individual and organizational performance. There are a number of schools that have, by any measurement—academics, climate, safety, attendance—terrible performance. "But my people are really excellent," the leader insists. Conversely, there are scores of schools with the superficial indicators of successful performance in the form of high test scores that greet with a blank stare the question, "What will you do differently next year to improve?"

The Essential Role: Making Connections

Organizations commonly have hard-working and committed leaders. Indeed, the leader may be at the point of exhaustion, noting the increasing hours while knowing a deep sense of compassion and commitment. Yet the leader is working exceedingly hard at the wrong things. No matter how many hours the architect works, the building does not rise from plans. No matter how passionate and diligent the architect is about the building, it does not grow from intention alone. The architect does something that no one else in the business process does, and I am not referring to drawing pictures and making plans. The seminal contribution of the architect is not merely creativity and design, but making connections among all the other contributors to the project. The building owners, community design authorities, construction supervisors, contractors, and a legion of inspectors all interact with the architect.

The connections made by the successful leader endure, just as the building does, long after the architect has departed the science. You have never heard someone express the fear, "It's a pretty good building, but once the architect leaves town, I'm afraid it will fall down." In a typical leadership situation, however, the concern is frequently expressed that the impact of successful leadership is transitory. Neither individual nor organizational success can endure, the theory goes, without the presence of the leader. If we wish to consider the impact of a leader of enduring quality, we should consider not the results of the past year but rather the impact that this leader had two, five, and ten years ago. These references, which appear to be dated to most people who conduct job interviews, might have the most insightful commentary on the enduring impact of the leader.

Results Are Not Enough

A common platitude in leadership literature is that the good leader is the one who gets results. Although results in the form of student achievement, organizational climate, safety, and staff morale are certainly important, they are an insufficient description of effective leadership. Our myopic focus on results allows us to obscure the more important and less noticed causes that precede those results. The leaders of many high-tech firms produced spectacular results in the form of rising stock price, but lacking profits, assets, and sustainability. The illusory results stemmed not from the skills of the corporate leader but from external market forces that elevated stories over substance.

School can also show short-term results from changes in student population; the smaller the school or class, the greater the impact of a small change can be. The typical error is comparing this year's fourth grade results to last year's fourth grade results and labeling the difference between those two numbers an indicator of the quality of the teacher and principal. Of course, in most cases, the two groups comprised entirely different children, and such comparison is unwarranted. More to the point, if a school wants to have higher scores, then it can do so by having the students with the greatest academic challenges drop out, or (in an increasing number of cases) having them receive an inaccurate and inappropriate special education label along with a recommendation for adaptation or exclusion from the test. That is not leadership, but gamesmanship in which genuine student success is sacrificed on the altar of results (Gardner, 1999).

The Antecedents of Excellence

As the architect of individual and organizational success, the effective leader engages in a continuing quest to identify, understand, and replicate the antecedents of excellence. Understanding of the antecedents of excellence on the one hand and mere existence in close proximity to successful results on the other is the essence of the difference between the leader who is effective and the one who is lucky. Some antecedents are obvious:

- If attendance improves, student achievement improves.
- If student nutrition improves, attention in class improves.
- If parental support in the form of reviewing homework, daily reading with students, and communicating clearly with teachers improves, then student achievement improves.

Other antecedents of excellence are less intuitive and raise important questions:

- If we increase the number of extracurricular activities, does this divert resources away from essential academic needs, or does it improve student attendance and thus improve academic achievement?
- If we increase professional development funding, does it give teachers and administrators vital skills for improved performance, or does it merely take them out of the building and reduce their contact with their students?
- If we increase our investment in technology, does it give students the skills they need in the twenty-first century, or amount to one more diversion from the academic essentials of the day?

The answers to these questions are typified by opinion rather than evidence. The central thesis of this book is that leaders practice the critical thinking disciplines we attempt to impart to elementary school students: they grasp the difference between fact and opinion. For the effective leader, the foregoing questions do not receive an immediate rejoinder in the form of a belief shaped by casual conversation supported by opinion and resting firmly on a foundation of prejudgment. Rather, the effective leader responds, accurately, "I don't know; let's gather some data so that we can better understand those relationships, test our preconceptions, and formulate some supportable answers."

Here, then, is the stark contrast in definitions of the effective leader. In one corner, there is the confident (read: bellicose and loquacious) leader who knows the answers; bullies his troops into submission; is popular; and feeds into the stereotype of military, business, and even educational leaders about whom premature biographies are written. He (the stereotypical strong leader is almost invariably male) is barely distinguishable from the schoolyard bully, whose bravado exceeds his competence, as his successor inevitably points out with a flourish. In the other corner, there is the leader whose effectiveness stems from learning rather than from pretending to have all the answers. This leader regularly answers "I don't know" and does not fear the embarrassing consequences of having one's presuppositions upended.

Grasping an understanding of the antecedents of excellence is not the result of attending conventions and conferences, nor the insight afforded by a video or book. It is the hard work of discovery, precisely the same work we expect of our students as they learn to read, explain a proof, or balance a chemical equation. Because it has been a long time since most adults have engaged in this awkward journey of error, trial, error, and eventual discovery, the memory of the joy of the insight may be faint, but the memory persists. You could not have learned to read this page without having encountered such a moment many times in your life. The effective leader recreates those moments regularly, not through instant wisdom and profound judgment but through questions, errors, admission of ignorance, persistent investigation, and eventual discovery. This book is not a set of answers, but the invitation to this essential voyage of discovery.

The Equity Imperative

Two centuries ago, Africans were enslaved and their rights in any state were largely a fiction. One hundred years ago, we no longer had slavery, though "separate but equal" was the law of the land and people spoke with casual righteousness of the "white man's burden." At the dawn of a new century, how far have we progressed? As

I write this, there is clear and persistent evidence about the differences in academic opportunity and achievement between Anglo and non-Anglo students, yet a curious debate rages in many school systems as to reporting the gap in performance between minority and majority children. This is the logic of the alcoholic who reasons that "If I don't count the number of drinks I have had today, then it must not be too bad."

During the past decade of working with educational leaders across the globe, I have adopted a rule that has served me well and saved a great deal of time: I spend all day and all night discussing, researching, and learning strategies for improving the performance of students, teachers, and leaders. I do not spend a single second discussing whether to improve performance. Once we have begun the "whether" conversation about the performance of children who are poor, whose skin contains melanin, whose parents are unemployed, or who acquire and process information differently from other children, then we have descended into the region of doubt and excuse. In this cloudy territory, the focus is not on how adults can improve but on clinical dissection of the faults of the children.

The architect does not despair about the inadequacies of the carpenters but instead creates a vision that is so clear and engaging that we build a place we and our kids will call home. The architect does not give up because the electrician, on a previous job, missed a connection but instead creates specifications that combine clarity of expectation with relentless optimism. My brother, Stephen, now a leader in the U.S. military chemical and biological defense effort, once described marriage as the triumph of hope over experience, an aphorism he tossed off despite his three decades of successful marriage to Katy. How little did he know that his description was supremely appropriate to his responsibilities in protecting a vulnerable nation. Even as a general, he is a soldier, responding to the call of duty when all logic would scream for him to run.

An effective educational leader must be both general and soldier, a leader who is simultaneously obedient to her values. Defending the nation from an unseen enemy does not make sense. Leading a school where children do not speak English, parents are not supportive, and safety is not guaranteed does not make any more sense than attempting to protect a nation from an enemy that is invisible with weapons that are calamitous in their consequences. As my brother would say, "Soldier on."

Values and Principles: A Harbor During the Inevitable Storm

It is easy for me to say "soldier on" when you are sitting at a desk with a literal or figurative bullet hole in it. Clark Lovell, an inspiring leader in his career at the Milwaukee public schools, took a desk with him from one assignment to the next; it had a bullet hole in it. This vivid symbol suggested, "Nothing you can say or do is more difficult or challenging than what I have already endured." You need not have a bullet hole in your desk to feel fear and anxiety. School leaders can count on shifting political winds, changing priorities, and conflicting counsel. How, then, do they know how to persist in the face of danger? How do they soldier on?

What are your fundamental values and principles? The question does not refer to an externally imposed list created by sacred texts of world religions or imperatives from influential teachers. In the absence of any externally imposed requirements—no state standards, no regulations, no parental or mentor expectations, no tests, no inspections—what would you do in response to the singular requirement of your values and principles? Most leaders I have interviewed on this point eventually respond tentatively, as if leading a school on the basis of values and principles rather than devotion to standardized tests and regulatory compliance is unthinkable. With some prodding, however, they ultimately offer the hope that they would lead a school or system of schools that is

- Creative
- Engaging
- Fun
- Respectful

- Rigorous
- Full of reading, writing, thinking, and reasoning

Here is the best news in this book: commitment to your values is neither iconoclastic nor a rejection of the rules and tests with which we must live every day. A leader who understands the antecedents of excellence finds techniques that are both related to desired results and consistent with personal values. For example, the leader who is committed to an academic environment that is "creative; engaging; fun; respectful; rigorous; and full of reading, writing, thinking, and reasoning" is not doomed to low test scores because this leader failed to enumerate curriculum goals and academic standards as part of the goals for this ideal school. Rather, the leader allows data analysis and not mindless tradition be the guide to applying these ideals to an educational environment in which students are creative and responsive to new ideas from ancient and modern texts, passionately engaged in their individual pursuits and willing to investigate subjects offered by teachers, and respectful of one another's need for emotional safety and challenging themselves and their peers to excel.

This vision of educational leadership is not, in sum, a transaction between merchant and customer, in which each tries to get the better of the bargain through commitment to the least cost. Rather, this model challenges the leader and every other participant in the educational system to identify and pursue values. This model emphasizes effectiveness rather than popularity. This model of leadership, more than anything, recognizes that our responsibility for students extends for more than six hours a day, 180 days a year; it represents a lifetime commitment of leadership and learning. In the next chapter, we explore how the transition to educational standards requires change, how individuals and organizations resist change, and how you can create effective change without exhausting yourself by attempting to overcome every obstacle during this long and challenging journey.

Chapter Two

The Leadership Dilemma

Building Consensus or Creating Change?

Leadership Keys

Change is essential

Consensus does not mean unanimity

Understand the sources of individual and organizational
 resistance

Build change champions

Celebrate small wins

Create a data-friendly environment

Change with a "pebble in the pond"

Choose how to spend the last ten minutes of your day

If we used the bell curve as our guide to leadership success, then
only 49.9 percent of people buying this book really need it. After
all, these are the hapless folks who are "below average" and hence
in need of a raft of prescriptions to help them. If, on the other
hand, we approach leadership from the perspective of standards,
then every educational organization in the world must acknowledge the need for improvement as there is not a single one that
uniformly produces completely exemplary results. Moreover,
because the very nature of an educational organization is that the
people involved in it are lifelong learners, there is always a distance
between our achievement today and our potential tomorrow.

I devote a good deal of my professional life to working with
school systems that suffer from the effects of multigenerational

poverty and low academic achievement. There is never a problem in discussing whether change is necessary in such an environment, though an astonishing amount of time is wasted on discussing whether change is possible. Several times each year, however, I visit school systems that have strikingly high achievement, as represented by an average percentile rank that places the student body in the top 20 percent nationally. "We're in the 80th percentile again this year, so we really don't have much to worry about," they claim. With the growth of standards-referenced assessment, however, the leadership challenge becomes quite different.

The complacency in these districts cannot be justified on the basis of their test scores—which are, relative to neighboring districts, quite good when one looks at the mean, or average, test score. Rather, they must look at another metric, the percentage of students who meet or exceed standards. It is not uncommon at all to find a high-performing district that boasts an average percentile rank of 80 and yet is surprised to discover that 40 percent of students do not meet their academic content standards. How can this be?

Using Standards to Defeat Complacency

The paradox of the district that simultaneously has a high percentile average score and a high percentage of students who fail to meet standards can be quickly understood if we recognize the inaccuracy of the bell curve to describe student achievement. Consider the mythical data of Figure 2.1, in which the average of the 80th percentile is neatly distributed in a symmetrical manner around the average. A few students are higher than the 80th percentile, a few students are lower, and most students are right at the average. Everyone can be tucked into bed at night firm in the conviction that, as Garrison Keillor assures us about Lake Wobegon, "All the children are above average."

Figure 2.1. Normal Distribution with Mean of 80

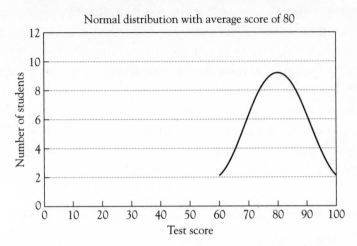

When the actual data are analyzed, however, another picture emerges. The same average percentile rank of 80 can represent an entirely different set of results, as Figure 2.2 indicates.

Technically, this distribution is bimodal, with a large number of students populating two places on the continuum of scores. I prefer the more descriptive term "camel hump" distribution. There is one

Figure 2.2. Bimodal ("Camel Hump") Distribution

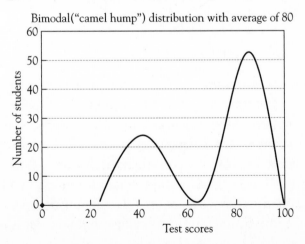

hump of the camel at the far right side of the scores, indicating a significant number of students who scored in the nineties, and a significant number of students who are in the thirties and forties. If we look only at the average of eighty, we can be complacent. If we get the story behind the numbers, we find a shockingly large number of students who are not meeting academic standards and who need decisive leadership attention. With each passing year, these differences widen; they are typically unmasked only late in high school, when unsuccessful students have dropped out, inflicting a lifetime of costs on themselves, their families, and society.

Dealing with the Failed Change Initiatives of the Past

This creates the leader's greatest challenge: individual and organizational change. In a high-performing district, many people think that change is unnecessary. In a low-performing district, many people think that change is not possible. In any organization, people know that change is uncomfortable. Finally, every one of your colleagues has witnessed change initiatives that have failed. Against this seemingly insurmountable set of psychological, organizational, historical, and logistical odds, we expect the educational leader to become the architect of successful change (De Pree, 1992; Benfari, 1999). Such a task is not impossible, but it is complex, difficult, and challenging intellectually and emotionally.

Why Is Change so Difficult?

M. Scott Peck, M.D., opened his international best-seller *The Road Less Traveled* with the words, "Life is difficult." The leader who bears the responsibility of transforming an organization must confront one of the most challenging parts of a difficult life: change. If life is difficult, as Peck observes, then surely one of the most difficult parts of life is abandoning the certain past to embrace an uncertain future. Change represents abandoning the past in pursuit of an uncertain future, and it is change that a leader is most frequently required to pursue. Few educational leaders are given the charge, "Everything here is running just fine, so please don't make any changes." Far more common is the requirement that the leader move the organization in a new direction, shake things up, build staff morale, and of course improve performance. Soon the leader recognizes that painless change is an oxymoron.

When confronted with a mandate for change, the best leaders do not resort to a sophomoric pep rally, or convenient slogan, or seductive mantra offered by the theory du jour. They recognize that if Peck's wisdom ("life is difficult") has merit, then change is exponentially more difficult. Effective leaders know that their task is not to render a difficult task simple, but rather to render successful accomplishment of a difficult task more rewarding than avoidance of the task. In brief, the pain of change and accompanying rewards of inertia must be exceeded by the rewards of change and the concomitant pain associated with business as usual.

The Human Equation and the Motivation for Change

The term *human equation* has been used in various contexts by scholars and philosophers. Pfeffer (1998) uses the term to advocate the primacy of human capital in organizational performance. My son Brooks, an observer of human behavior who is wise beyond his years, offers an alternative understanding of the human equation that has allowed me to rethink the issue. Most views of the relationship between organizations and people rely on the behaviorist principle, which is, at best, a Newtonian fantasy of human relations: for every action by the organization, there is a reaction by the individual. The fantasy is not that the individual responds to organizational decisions, but that the organization can manipulate both parts of this interaction. Once we accept that the individual's reaction is neither identical nor manageable, we can see that the real human equation is that individuals and organizations seek to maximize reward and minimize pain.

This simple equation has profound implications for the leader. Change does not occur as a result of a splendid new strategic plan, richly bound in leather, and announced with effusive pride at a staff meeting. Change does not occur as a result of inviting a motivational speaker who beguiles the audience into laughter and tears. Change does not occur because of administrative directives. Change does not occur because of new scheduling. Change in individuals and organizations only occurs if there is conscious recognition that the human equation governs individual and collaborative decisions.

In brief, our change strategies must explicitly address the question "What's in it for me?" and offer a clear and direct answer. This is neither mercenary nor cynical, but a recognition of how individuals and organizations make decisions. Moreover, the response to the question "What's in it for me?" need not imply a pecuniary reward. Successful educators and school leaders can gain financial reward outside of the profession. Nevertheless, we are all amenable to the influence of meaningful rewards, including greater freedom and autonomy, professional growth opportunities, improved working environment, and more time to prepare for the complexities of classroom work. Conversely, we react strongly to noneconomic sanctions, including reduction in control of our work and reduced professional independence, constricted opportunities for professional growth, a toxic work environment that includes both physical and relationship elements that are counterproductive, and the burdens of more tasks with fewer hours to prepare to accomplish those tasks well.

Equity Is Not Equality

One important trait of effective leaders is their recognition that the value in fair treatment of all of their colleagues does not require identical treatment with respect to these noneconomic rewards and sanctions. Indeed, the leader committed to equity constantly uses a variety of incentives—allocation of rewards and sanctions, encouragement and recognition, direction and freedom from direction, provision of time and restriction of freedom—all in a manner that meets the individual needs of people in the organization. For greater elaboration on the principles of equitable leadership, two excellent resources are *First, Break All the Rules* (Buckingham and Coffman, 1999) and *Situational Leader* (Hersey, 1992).

Value Implications of the Human Equation

When leaders accept and understand the human equation, they are not substituting manipulation for principle. Rather, applying the human equation to leadership challenges conveys respect for the fundamental principle that individual needs have value and personal fears deserve consideration. Most important, the observation that we all consider an increase in reward and a reduction in pain to be a good thing is not a statement of values, but merely an observation of truth. Newton does not ask if we like gravity, nor does Einstein inquire about the impact of relativity on human values. Physical principles just exist, and the behavior of bodies, from planets to atomic particles, is consistent with those principles.

Such a clinical view of humanity as seeking reward and avoiding pain may be unpleasant in a world that prefers the illusion of pure altruism—and particularly in the world of education, where pursuit of reward is frequently regarded with suspicion and acceptance of pain a badge of honor. The human equation holds that even if people voluntarily submit to pain (as with protestors who are arrested or employees who are fired as a result of failing to comply with a requirement they believe to be immoral), then whatever pain is associated with the penalty of arrest or unemployment is less than the pain of submission to authority. Thus even in a case of altruism, sacrifice, or self-denial on the basis of a moral principle, the human equation is consistent with the behavior of the vast majority of our species.

In the context of educational leadership, the human equation has profound implications. Change in individual and organizational behavior occurs only when the members of the organization perceive a change in the reward and pain associated with change. Because any change, any disruption of routine, any departure from the comfortable involves some pain, then the leader must create a reward that more than counterbalances the pain of change. In the alternatives, the leader must make clear that the price of stagnation entails pain that is greater than that associated with the proposed change (Ciampa and Watkins, 1999). Such a view forces the leader to take a far more analytical view of the implications of change.

The Implications of Change

The implications of change vary strikingly with the perspective of the person rendering the analysis. Here are some comments on a change to standards-based education, all in the same school:

"Finally we'll have some clarity around here, and we don't have to guess what student success is supposed to mean."

"Are you telling me that everything I've been doing for twenty-eight years is wrong? That all my teaching awards and letters of commendations were a fraud?"

"I'm already doing this, so there's no need for me to do anything differently."

"Yeah, right, whatever. I'm seen a new initiative each year for the last ten years, and this too shall pass."

"I've labored for years to create this curriculum. I guess you don't need me anymore."

"Colleagues used to ask me for help on student achievement issues, but I guess that standards provide all the answers now."

"Publish any standards you want. Once the classroom door closes, it's my show."

"I can't influence what happens in the classroom. If I do, I'll get a union grievance."

Leaders reading this book have heard all of these objections and many more. They hear them with such regularity that they are tempted to cringe and react abruptly: "Look—it's nonnegotiable, so just do it." As frequently, demoralized and defeated faculty members say half-heartedly, "Just tell me what to do so I can get it over with." Domination and submission are not the elements of effective leadership. In fact, one of the most critical roles every leader plays is that of teacher (Tichy, 1997; Ackerman, Donaldson, and Van Der Bogert, 1996). We do not want our students to become submissive to mathematics, but to understand and apply the discipline. We do not achieve our goals by yelling that "Topic sentences are nonnegotiable!" Rather, we give students the power of written communication that makes conventions of grammar, usage, and expression something they embrace. In this context, teaching and learning takes time, and so it is when leaders teach their colleagues about new values, visions, principles, and techniques.

Rather than react in an argumentative or dismissive fashion to objections of this sort, a leader can begin with the premise that all of these reactions are common and understandable. People perceive change not in an organizational context but in an individual one. Whether or not they articulate the question, their varying analyses of the implications of change make clear that they are asking, "What does this mean for me?" The wise leader does not regard these challenges as the first round in an endless debate, but rather as an opportunity for investigation and discovery.

I have found it useful to begin a session involving discussion of academic standards by asking the audience to complete the sentence, "Standards will not work here because. . . ." I carefully note each objection on a large piece of paper and place it on the wall. During the break, people are invited to add to the list. In addition, if an objection has been satisfactorily answered, the person who entered it has the opportunity to strike through the entry, so that I can focus on those objections that are most troublesome. With uncanny similarity, seminars follow a diamond-shaped pattern in which the number of objections rises slowly and then grows rapidly, almost to the point of discouragement. But then the list starts to decline, as one objection after another falls. The objections are not removed by way of a speaker winning debating points with the person who posed the objection. It is the participants, not the seminar leader, who remove an objection. There is a critical lesson here. Leaders do not remove objections by fiat but through teaching, learning, shared vision, and mutual ownership.

First Why, Then How

Reaction to the implications of change tends to be egocentric. The implication is that I did something wrong, that I am inadequate, and I will have to work more; my work is not valued. In discussing the rationale for change, the leader can quickly become stuck in playing a therapeutic role with colleagues. Rather than becoming bogged down in a role that is unproductive and inappropriate, the leader is better advised to move the rationale for change away from an egocentric discussion (Barth, 1990). In other words, it isn't just about me, and it isn't just about you; nor is the imperative for change about any individual person.

The "Absence of Change" Myth

Resistance to change implies that there is a choice between changing and not changing. This is a myth. If an educational organization is considered from a systems perspective, the absence of change is not an option. Even in the case where individuals within the system remain steadfastly committed to the status quo (bronzed lecture notes, tried-and-true classroom activities, immutable leadership practices), it is not accurate to say that these individuals are stuck in an unchanged system. In fact, the system changes every day as students, communities, the economy, the culture, and the world all make changes, some of which are incremental and some of which are violent and dramatic.

The fact that one element of that system fails to change does not prevent the system from changing; each time the system changes, the relationships among the elements of the system also change. Thus the entire concept that we have a choice between change and no change is an illusion. In fact, we can only choose either to change wisely on the basis of clear direction, careful analysis of data, and commitment to fundamental values; or to change unwisely, on the basis of whim, chance, prejudgment, and guesses from the results of a fact-free debate.

There are many elements of the educational universe that have changed in the past decade. Eavesdrop on the conversation of any meeting of educators, administrators, or parents, and you will notice abundant observations on the myriad ways in which students, curriculum, and governance have changed. Each of those changes has an impact on the other people in the system, including leaders and teachers. It is those changes—not just changes in individual behavior—that are the reason we need to also change our organizational approach to academic achievement.

The Consensus Conundrum

As the "test doctor" of the Internet for almost a decade now, I receive eighty to ninety questions each day from school leaders, board members, teachers, parents, and students. In the course of more than eighty keynote speeches each year, I receive a number of questions from the floor. Despite the large quantity of questions that I hear, the similarities are remarkable. Without doubt, the most frequent one I hear from school leaders is, "How do we get buy-in for innovation?" The implication is that successful innovation must be popular, and that the effective leader invariably uses consensus as the best model for decision making. The consensus model has become so commonplace that few people challenge it. It is, after all, much easier to lead a group when everyone agrees with the decisions, isn't it? The implication is that the best leadership is also the easiest. Both of these implications of the consensus model—elevation of popularity over effectiveness and ease over difficulty—deserve a second look.

Although I would not make a case for the arbitrary and capricious leader, I would challenge the notion of leadership effectiveness that accepts the criteria of popularity with colleagues and lack of stress on the job (Hargrove, 1998; Calkins, 1994). In two recent instances, I had the opportunity to observe educational leaders discussing the deplorable state of literacy among their children. They considered their options, most notably expansion of the amount of time devoted to teaching children to read. To my astonishment, these experienced and well-respected school leaders said, "Of course, we can't possibly do this unless there is buy-in from all of my staff." There were nods of agreement around the room.

Only a couple of us challenged this presumption. "Wait a minute!" we interjected. "Are you saying that if one faculty member prefers to continue doing things the way you have in the past, you won't give your kids the additional literacy assistance that they need?"

"We've tried the top-down approach in the past and it just doesn't work," they explained. "If you don't have faculty buy-in, you just can't get anything done."

This conversation made me wonder what would happen if one day the food service workers decided that the most recent hygiene requirements were just a passing fad and that, as a matter of personal freedom, they would decide not to buy in to those requirements. Or what if the school nurse and other health workers did not buy in to the vaccination requirements for students? One can only hope that there are values of health and safety greater than these leaders' needs for consensus. The essential question is whether there are educational issues that rise to the level of "health and safety" and thus are so important that universal popularity is no longer the criterion for acceptance. In view of the enormous costs to the individual and society when students fail in school, a persuasive argument can be made that student success, and particularly student literacy, is a health-and-safety issue.

Change Without Consensus

Leaders are human, and it is understandable that they want to be popular with their colleagues. The consensus model of leadership, however, renders the process of making a decision more important than the decision itself. Because educational leaders must ultimately focus on their core values and the children served, there are times when consensus is neither necessary nor appropriate. Values, not popularity, should govern educational policy. The use of values does not imply a heavy-handed dictatorial approach to leadership. The effective leader always explains the rationale for a decision and equips colleagues with the knowledge and skills necessary to be successful in every task. But the notion that the effective leader also ensures that every decision is popular—or, worse yet, that a single dissenting voice on a faculty is sufficient to scuttle a necessary initiative—is a prescription for failure.

Suggesting that values are more important than popular assent is heresy in contemporary leadership circles. This is a throwback to the "theory X" style of the 1950s, in which leadership demands were premised on a lack of trust of the factory workers, whose every move must be managed and directed. The more enlightened "theory Y" managers were able to create self-directed teams and, most of all, were imbued with a fundamental humanitarian vision of the workplace that their Neanderthal theory X counterparts failed to achieve. Much of the leadership literature suggested that although mere managers handle tasks and goals, real leaders work with loftier visions and principles. The implication was mutual exclusivity between the two terms, and there was no doubt that leaders were superior to and more enlightened than managers.

When an organization must change—and every organization must change at one time or another—then its leaders must be guided by vision and principles, but they must also manage the tasks at hand. Their job is not merely to persuade and cajole their colleagues to do the work at hand but also to ensure that the essential tasks are accomplished (Ulrich, Zenger, and Smallwood, 1999;

Useem, 1998). I will do my best to educate cafeteria workers about the need for hygiene practices and build internal motivation for maintaining a healthy and safe food service area, but at the end of the day I do not care if the people serving food to my students *like* washing their hands. Perhaps in due course, as quality increases and inspection results show excellent performance, washing hands will not be a controversial issue. But we start with the essential behavior; we do not wait for it to become popular, nor do we give a second thought to the need for consensus on the matter.

Let's return to the example of the need for improved literacy. The evidence is absolutely clear in a majority of schools in the nation: a substantial percentage of students do not have the reading skills that allow them to be successful at the next grade. Writing results are even more dismal, with some estimates ranging as high as 70 percent of students not having the skills to communicate in writing that are necessary for their grade level. We have the academic equivalent of dirty hands in the cafeteria line, yet when the vocabulary changes from hygiene to literacy, educational leaders are paralyzed. Consensus, rather than common sense, is the criterion for the decision.

It is important to note that this is not a controversy over whether students should study *Julius Caesar* or *Moby Dick*. This is a controversy over whether children's need to read is more important than the personal desire of those who find change inconvenient. To understand how an organization becomes mired in inertia, it is important to understand the two types of resistance to change that the leader must confront. These are organizational resistance and individual resistance to virtually any change effort.

Organizational Resistance to Change

An organization ought to be an inert being, composed of nothing but the sum of the individuals in it. But as anyone who has worked in an organization knows, there are other institutional factors at work, among them tradition, history, and feelings that have been nurtured or bruised from age-old controversy. Each new innovation faces potential resistance not merely from individuals but also from the system of relationships that have developed over time. Even if the proposed change is not resisted by an individual, it almost always has an impact on systemic relationships that involve the individual. For example, it may appear that the academic standards movement has the greatest impact on teachers. But school counselors, library media center specialists, as well as special area teachers in art, music, physical education, and foreign language all have been affected by the standards movement.

Sometimes the impact is positive, as in those schools that have used standards as an opportunity to make every adult in the building an educator of children, taking personal responsibility for student success. In other cases, the impact has been unpredictable and negative, as when standards are equated with testing and the focus of attention therefore rests only on the grades and subjects that are tested. This alienates the teachers, who feel as if they are under the microscope from those who escape such scrutiny, and widens the gulf between the teachers whose subjects appear as a score in the newspaper for all to see and those whose performance remains hidden from public view.

Individual Resistance to Change

Individual resistance to change is inevitable. Let me repeat that: individual resistance to change is inevitable. A leader who makes universal buy-in the price of any innovation is doomed to stagnation (Goodlad, 1994; Anderson, 2001); he might make dissent sufficiently unpopular that it is only expressed when he is out of earshot, but this does not eliminate individual resistance. The leader might make resistance go underground, but he does not eliminate it. Thus the only rational method for the leader to deal with individual resistance to change is to identify it, accept it for what it is, and move on.

Individual resistance to change may stem from several causes, notably disbelief in the effectiveness of the proposed change, or a set of personal experiences that make the proposed changes appear unwise, or a fear of personal impact that can range from inconvenience to embarrassment. Each cause of individual resistance can be dealt with respectfully and effectively if it is accurately identified. For example, if there is disbelief in the effectiveness of the proposed change, it is reasonable for the leader to help the resisting colleagues express their views as a hypothesis. Using the typical "if, then" format, a hypothesis might state, "If this change is enacted, then student achievement will decline" or "If this change is enacted, then it will rob time from other areas and cause those important programs to decline." Using the hypothesis-testing model, we can move from emotional argument to rational analysis of the data.

For example, the leader might propose an increase in the amount of time devoted to student writing, an initiative that is supported by a great deal of evidence but that remains generally unpopular with teachers. It is not that teachers are resistant to the evidence of the impact of good writing; rather, they are well aware of the multiple demands on time in their day and the incessant requirements that they cover many other academic subjects in addition to writing. Because writing is quite time-consuming for both students and teachers, the time devoted to writing is, they argue, time taken away from some other equally essential subject. At first, the resistance to the leader's initiative might sound like this: "We can't do this writing program—it takes too much time and we just don't have any more time!" Upon further inquiry, we can find the hypothesis that is behind the statement.

In fact, "We don't have the time" is never a true statement, unless the clocks and calendars in the location of the complainant are remarkably different from the twenty-four-hour day, seven-day week observed elsewhere around the world. The common contention of insufficient time is actually the statement of a hypothesis: if we spend more time on writing, then we will have less time to devote to other areas, and therefore our performance in those other areas (math, science, social studies) will decline.

We have now transformed a complaint into a hypothesis. Complaints lead to argument; hypotheses lead to testing. Perhaps the hypothesis is true. If so, the data supporting the hypothesis should look something like the graph in Figure 2.3. On the horizontal axis, the leader has plotted the time devoted to student writing; on the vertical axis, the leader has plotted the results of tests in math, science, and social studies. As the hypothesized graph indicates, more time on writing leads to lower scores on the other subjects, presumably because those other subjects were robbed of time that was squandered on writing.

When confronted with a hypothesis, a leader does not respond with rapier wit, clever debating points, or administrative dogma. Hypotheses cannot be tested with leadership charisma; they can only be tested with data. In this particular example, a number of researchers (Calkins, 1994; Darling-Hammond, 1997; Reeves, 2000c) have found that the hypothesis that writing hurts performance in other areas is unsupported by the data. Thus the response to the hypothesis is simply comparison of the hypothesized data analysis of Figure 2.3 with the actual data of Figure 2.4, which shows that the actual data are the opposite of the hypothesis.

Figure 2.3. Common Hypothesis About the Impact of Writing

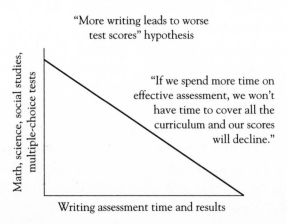

"More writing leads to worse test scores" hypothesis

"If we spend more time on effective assessment, we won't have time to cover all the curriculum and our scores will decline."

Math, science, social studies, multiple-choice tests

Writing assessment time and results

Figure 2.4. Testing Hypotheses with Data

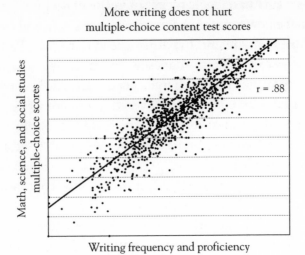

More writing does not hurt
multiple-choice content test scores

Note well that presenting data does not invalidate the individual who offered resistance to the leader's program; it only tests one hypothesis. This creates an environment of mutual respect and an ethic that data, rather than administrative fiat, will resolve contentious issues. These are not personal victories or defeats, but simply shared commitment to truth. The real test of the integrity of this approach is when, more than a few times, the leader's own hypotheses are tested and found wanting, and the leader announces without a moment's hesitation, "It looks as if I was wrong, and I'm very glad that we tested this hypothesis and learned something from it. After all, as the researchers say, we learn more from error than from uncertainty. Now that we have tested this hypothesis, what other ideas can we explore and test in the same way?"

In addition to belief in an alternative hypothesis, other sources of individual resistance are personal experience and fear of personal inconvenience or embarrassment. Personal experience, extending to childhood, is a powerful backdrop that forms the basis of today's firmly held beliefs. This is particularly true in education, where the vast majority of people formed their judgments about the matter not from reading research but from recalling the most vivid experiences of their own childhood. Rather than allow differing recollections to dissolve into an unproductive "'tis-'tain't" controversy, the leader can deal with personal experience and fear in an analytical and humane manner. For example, before discussing a standards-based approach to evaluating student work, it might be useful for the leader to allow each faculty member to share one of her most vivid memories of grading and evaluation from when she was a student. This powerful recollection helps all parties to the discussion understand that there are emotions at work, and though emotions should not trump data in a policy debate, a leader errs gravely in being dismissive of the power of emotional history. By recalling and discussing memories of an evaluative experience that a teacher had in her own student days, the leader is able to help the entire team recognize where emotional connections are interfering with rational analysis of student achievement.

Emotional Sources of Resistance

The final source of individual resistance is fear and embarrassment. This is rarely articulated by either leader or colleague, because the mere suggestion that there might be fear and embarrassment as factors in the discussion seems accusatory ("What do I have to be afraid of? I've been a successful teacher for eighteen years!"). If we let our defenses down, however, it turns out that leaders and educators alike have several fears, and our unwillingness to discuss them does not render the fear any less powerful. Once a safe environment has been created, I hear comments such as these:

> Even though I've been teaching a long time, I realize that I'm a master of my curriculum. Now that the state has adopted academic standards, the honest truth is that there are things in there that I just don't know. The standards make me feel stupid. I'm a master teacher, and now I feel dumb in front of my colleagues, my principal, and even my students. It's awful.

I'm the best math teacher in the city, bar none. My students have gone to Ivy League schools and have excelled. My kids regularly get credit for college calculus courses, and I helped build the foundation for that. But you know what? I'm a lousy writer, and now that the administration wants to do writing across the curriculum, I will no longer be the great math teacher, but just one more lousy writing teacher. I hate being incompetent at anything, and I can't stand to be embarrassed in front of my colleagues.

I've been the principal of this school for seven years. It's a safe place, with a great faculty and good kids. I devote a lot of time to building parent relationships and supporting my faculty members. Nobody seems to notice, but I also balance a $2.6 million budget every year and always get a clean audit, I've never had a grievance, and never had an equity complaint from personnel. But now I hear that the principal is supposed to facilitate collaborative assessment conferences. What the heck is that? I do all the things a principal is supposed to do and then some, but now with one more requirement, I find myself starting over again. This is humiliating.

The emotional pain and necessary honesty associated with each of these statements does not emerge in a climate of distrust or if the issue of the day is decided by the volume of argument rather than the content of the contention. Leaders who are too busy expressing their opinions and announcing their decisions never have the opportunity to hear the emotional roots of individual resistance. Their failure to hear this resistance does not make it disappear; it only forces resistance under the surface, where the damage is even greater. By contrast, a leader who is willing to hear individual resistance for what it is—alternative hypotheses, fear of the unknown, concern over potential embarrassment, or a reflection of past personal experience—risks taking a little more time to implement a decision. The risk is more than rewarded with insight and information, as well as the motivation that inevitably accompanies deep personal respect conveyed only by quiet and attentive listening to another person's point of view.

Recognizing and Supporting Change Champions

In every organization, there are those few people who seem to get it as if by osmosis. Before the leader suggests a new initiative, Anne has already read about it and is spreading enthusiasm among her colleagues. Before the leader has even heard of it, Larry is experimenting in the classroom and refining the next iteration of it. These professionals are the change champions who exist in almost every organization. Yet their efforts are frequently unrecognized. Leadership researcher Tom Peters (Peters and Austin, 1995) documented the success of "skunk works" whose efforts in unglamorous settings and unheralded achievements were able to create enormous results for their organizations. Mike Schmoker (2001) has identified similar successes among soft-spoken and unnoticed educational professionals.

In my own experience, I have noticed a few classrooms or schools that appear to perform strikingly better than others, and the superintendent appeared to be surprised. "He isn't somebody I would have thought of as one of our best teachers," one superintendent remarked, as he viewed the results of the fourth grade teacher who, with demographically similar students, achieved academic results that were by far the best in the district. That teacher's classroom was remarkably different as well, with students practicing daily what other fourth grade teachers did only a few times a year. The teacher, however, was not visible at public meetings either as a supporter or a complainer, but merely a quiet professional who achieved remarkable things in the classroom.

Change champions are not particularly popular. Their success takes away the excuses used by others to prove that success is impossible. Their enthusiasm and joy in their work is the rejoinder to the contention that hard work and concomitant success is dreary and painful. Their commitment to the work at hand and their conspicuous honesty makes them distinctly unsuccessful in the game of office politics. They aren't, after all, trying to impress the superintendent; they are trying to help their students learn. Thus the leader cannot wait for change champions to stand up and identify themselves. Leaders must make a proactive effort to identify and nurture change champions, and help them find one another. Because they may be isolated in a building or a district, change champions must find their own network, using conferences, professional development, leadership support, and the Internet as mechanisms to demonstrate that they are not alone.

Celebrate Small Wins

The learning leader does not wait for annual test results to celebrate student achievement. He finds more frequent opportunities—say, those days when the sun rises in the east. Change initiatives are typically too complex and too time-consuming, with goals that extend into years, if not decades. The goal of "100 percent student proficiency in persuasive writing" is laudable and even necessary, but the learning leader makes a point of celebrating each increment of progress toward that goal. Leadership researcher Jim Collins (2001) presents a useful illustration in the incubation of an egg. How silly it would be, he notes, if we were to observe the egg from the moment it was laid until the instant it was hatched, and then celebrate the hatching as an "accomplishment" that was vastly more important than any of the days that preceded it. Each step of development and each moment of nurturing were part of the achievement of the hatchling, and those antecedents were no less worthy of notice and admiration than the first chirp of the chick.

In the context of education, we are much better at celebrating the hatching than the nurturing. We stand and cheer for the valedictorian, many years after a seventh grade teacher intervened in the life of an unsteady adolescent. We marvel at the success of our sixth grader, apparently unaware that a kindergarten teacher initiated a reluctant learner into the joys of reading. The learning leader celebrates the first written words of a kindergartner with the same enthusiasm granted to the valedictorian. The learning leader applauds as much for the third grader whose attendance has improved and whose reading has opened new doors as for the high school football team that wins the state championship. There is nothing wrong with football games and championships; they teach us how to celebrate. The question is, Do we apply those lessons in joyous celebration to the less noticeable victories in the everyday classroom? Do we, in short, celebrate the small wins with the same energy as we invest in the more obvious victories?

Create a Data-Friendly Environment

One of the pioneers in the effective schools movement, Larry Lezotte, is famous for asking two questions that leave many listeners speechless: What are you learning today? How will you know if you are successful?

The number of students, teachers, and school leaders who can answer both questions is, even after decades of Lezotte's importuning, relatively small. It is not that we are unwilling to respond to these reasonable questions, but rather that we frequently lack the information with which to give a coherent response. "How will we know if we are successful?" he asks. If our response is a review of grade cards or final examination scores, then we are no better than the physician who examines the results of an autopsy to assess the health of a patient. Lezotte's questions cannot be answered with an autopsy. He wants to know what we have learned *today* and how we will know if we are successful *today*.

We cannot respond to this questioning with feelings or intuition. "I think the kids are doing OK," we might offer. "Yes, it went pretty well today," we add with a suggestion of hope. The question remains: "How do you know?" In fact, we do not—unless we regard data as our ally rather than a source of intimidation and embarrassment. To most educators and school leaders, the very word *data* conjures up test scores and the complexities of psychometric analysis. It need not be so. In the most data-friendly schools I have visited, there is no patina of statistical sophistication, but rather clear explication of the percentage of students who have met the most important academic standards. Moreover, the data gathered and analyzed do not apply only to the students.

A data-friendly environment indicates that children are not the only ones who have responsibilities that can be measured. Next to the chart of student attendance there is a chart that reveals staff attendance. Next to a chart of student performance in writing, there is a chart that displays the frequency with which teachers require writing in classroom assessments. Next to a chart of the performance of teachers, there is a chart showing the frequency with which the leader has recognized best practices among the professional staff. Next to the chart of leadership performance there is a chart showing the percentage of agenda items in the last school board meeting that focused on student achievement. Finally, there is a chart that displays the percentage of parents who have been actively involved in direct support of student achievement at the school.

A data-friendly environment, in other words, is not merely a school that measures and quantifies the activities of children. A data-friendly school uses numbers not as a weapon but as a guide. The data-friendly leader uses measurement not only to suggest how children can improve their performance but more important how the adults in the system can improve their leadership, teaching, and curriculum strategies.

Isn't there a risk that data can be wrong? Certainly. Isn't there a risk that the test scores don't tell the entire story? Of course. The possibility, indeed the certainty, of those errors forms the rationale for more data gathering, not less. As a cardinal principle of measurement, it is better to measure a few things many times to compensate for inevitable measurement error, than to attempt to measure many things only once each year. The fewer times we measure something, particularly something variable such as academic achievement, the greater the risk of measurement error and inaccurate inferences from that measurement. Thus a data-friendly environment accepts error as the inevitably human component of the educational enterprise. The response to this error is not the illusion of perfection or perpetual excuse making, but rather provision of multiple sources of measurement so that no observer—whether leader, policy maker, parent, or student—need rely on a single data source to draw an important conclusion.

Pebble in a Pond: An Alternative Vision of Change

Much has been written about the need for "systemic change," but it remains an illusion. At best, the leader might achieve what I would describe as "systemic compliance"—that is, a measurable increase in the number of people who complete a prescribed activity within a prescribed period of time. This is not at all the same as changing the professional practices of thousands of people within a system. The irony is not lost on those who contrast the language of the job interview with the frustration of a leader pursuing systemic change. During the interview, we seek people who are bright, creative, and independent. During the systemic change initiative a few weeks hence, we are dismayed to find so many people who are bright, creative, and independent.

There is a better way to view systemic change, and that is to acknowledge it is a myth. One of the best superintendents in the nation, Terry Thompson, recently noted, "We have been successful only here and there—how do we bring this success to scale?" The only answer I can offer is, "One classroom at a time." This is not what a driven and successful school leader wants to hear, but it is the only answer that makes any sense. Change does not occur as it does in a marching band, where the drum major gives a signal and, in a quarter of a beat, the entire unit is transformed. It is far more likely that change occurs like a pebble in a pond. The first pebble cast into the water makes a few skips, and then settles into the pond with a few ripples around it. The second pebble lands in a slightly different place, making some additional ripples. Some of the ripples of the second pebble intersect with those of the first pebble, while other ripples enter new territory of the pond. But before too many pebbles have been cast into the pond, the number of ripples (and, even more, the number of intersecting ripples) is incalculable.

The metaphor is meaningful on several levels. First, the impact of successful change is not unidirectional; it expands in multiple directions with unintended and unnoticed impact. The physical education teacher notices the impact of writing on students, while the art teacher notices the relationship between his discipline and the academic standards for measurement, scale, and ratio. Meanwhile, the literature teacher notices that standards are hardly a new innovation but, on the basis of a serendipitous conversation with the soccer coach, finds that clear expectations that students understand, interpret, and apply have been integral to successful coaching practice for many years.

These insights, I regret to report, do not occur from an out-of-town consultant preaching the virtues of academic standards. Insight stems from observing, from comparing prejudgment with data, and from concluding that the prejudgment may be wanting. The learning leader does not create meaningful change by attempting to orchestrate a marching band, but by casting some pebbles into the pond. The ripples can be unpredictable and, in the most precise sense of the term, chaotic. Nevertheless, this is an accurate illustration of the process of organizational and individual change.

The Last Ten Minutes of the Leader's Day

Change is exhausting (Goleman, 1998; Parson, 1986). Having persisted to the end of this chapter, you may be exhausted as well. So let us assume that you have only ten minutes left at the end of this very long day. Your voice mail, e-mail, and in-box are all full. You are late, again, for dinner. You cannot possibly accomplish everything, so you pack your briefcase and head for your car. As you leave your office, there are two open doors on each side of the hallway. Inside one door is a colleague who has yet another argument to offer on why your initiatives are a waste of time—and, more to the point, an insult to the professional integrity of every experienced educator. Behind the other door is a little-noticed colleague who, without fanfare or accolade, has listened, responded, worked, and succeeded. In the ten minutes that separate the present instant from your departure from the parking lot, what will you do? Will you have one more fruitless argument with a malcontent, or will you nurture your change champion?

In an astonishing number of faculty meetings and professional development conferences, the conversation is defined by the malcontents, while the champions sit in silence, hoping only to return to their classrooms, where they can accomplish something constructive. You have ten minutes left. You have developed the perfect rhetorical stiletto for the malcontent. You have the oratorical skill to deliver it. You have the perfect time limit in which to launch the verbal missile and escape before the counterattack. Or, you can reject this aimless and vacuous contentiousness and walk into the second door. Your change champion, not expecting you, will be surprised and perhaps alarmed. For this person, you have no prepared speech, no rhetorical flourishes. But you can say, "I know that this isn't easy for you, but I want you to know that I notice it and I appreciate it. What you are doing for our kids is terrific, and I respect you a great deal. I'm on my way home, but would you mind telling me about the best thing that happened to you today?"

Now envision your walk to the parking lot, your drive to the house, and your evening at home. You only have ten minutes with which you can either argue with a malcontent or nurture a change champion. Choose wisely.

Chapter Three

The Leadership and Learning Matrix

Leadership Keys

Combine causes and effects in a Leadership and Learning Matrix

What Homer Simpson and Warren Buffet can teach us about leadership

Perfection is not an option

Luck is not a strategy

Leaders are not victims

Resilience is a choice

Apply the L^2 matrix to your own leadership decisions

Recent volumes on leadership assure the reader that Attila the Hun, Jesus, Lao-tzu, Moses, Patton, or Shakespeare, to name only a few, might have the keys to understanding the secrets of effective leadership. Consider a less intimidating figure: Homer Simpson. This creation of Matt Groening has done what few cartoon characters can claim in that his trademark expression, "D'oh!" has entered the text of the *Oxford English Dictionary*. With monosyllabic precision, Homer's expression encapsulates an important understanding of leadership effectiveness. First, the *OED* definition:

D'oh! Intj. Expressing frustration at the realization that things have turned out badly or not as planned or that one has just said or done something foolish.

The etymologist responsible for the insertion, John Simpson (presumably no relation to Homer), understands two distinct forces to be at work in this expression. The first is the bad result that frames Homer's every action during a typical episode of TV's *The Simpsons*. The second is Homer's indifferent ignorance to the causes of the bad result. This combination of bad results and absent understanding of the causes of those results embodies the lower-left quadrant of the Leadership and Learning (L²) Matrix, seen in Figure 3.1. On the vertical axis of the matrix is achievement of results, which might be profit, employee stability, customer satisfaction, patient health, fundraising success, or any among a variety of indicators important to an organization. On the horizontal axis is the leader's understanding of the cause of the results or the antecedents of excellence. When one has bad results without understanding, one does not find the intersection of ignorance and bliss; one finds *D'oh!*

Figure 3.1.   The Leadership and Learning (L²) Matrix

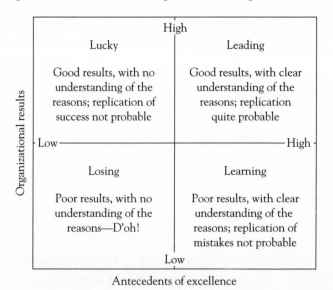

The Lucky Leader: Results Without Understanding

Above Homer's quadrant, we find the subject of much business journalism: the leader who coexisted with good results and thus was presumed to have caused them. Here one finds, for instance, "Chainsaw" Al Dunlap, formerly of Sunbeam, whose best-selling book extolled the virtues of massive layoffs while omitting mention that accounting frauds are seldom the hallmark of lasting financial success. Also in the quadrant that, at best, can be described as "lucky" are some of the dot-com billionaires who convinced a short-lived generation of investors that because today's stock price is higher than yesterday's, tomorrow's will inevitably follow suit. By such logic, trees grow to the sky.

This quadrant has a dark side, in which the leader presumes that present position is the result of eternal gifts. Tyrants from Louis XIV to Stalin reveled in the presumption that short-term success automatically validated their position, and that an understanding of underlying causality was irrelevant. When those who evaluate leaders indulge in a one-dimensional focus on results, they lose the opportunity for a multidimensional understanding of antecedents, often with tragic consequences.

Discovering the Value of Failures

In the lower-right quadrant, we have those who are apparent failures. After all, as their low position on the vertical axis indicates, success eludes them. But because these leaders understand the antecedents of excellence, their failures are temporary. During the technology boom of 1999, investment wizard Warren Buffet fell into this quadrant. Critics wondered if the world's second-richest man had lost his touch because he failed to follow the stampede into stocks whose stories had more imagination than earnings. Perhaps some of them wished that Buffet had invested in a hot Houston company named Enron; it certainly had better performance than the stodgy company from Omaha.

Buffett played his hand carefully, enduring the criticism with intellectual curiosity rather than defensiveness. "I do not invest where I do not understand," he said, and thus cast himself as the archetype of the learner. Today he counts his billions while his critics paper their bathroom walls with worthless stock certificates.

Perfection Is Not an Option

Who occupies the upper-right quadrant, where the leader achieves great results and understands the antecedents of success? History does not record a leader who occupied only this portion of the L^2 matrix. In fact, the knowledge that links results with understanding was probably gained during an apprenticeship in the learning quadrant. Buffet surely occupies not a quadrant but a continuum between learning and leading.

The L^2 matrix offers no pat solution, no historical figure of mythic proportions whose secrets reveal consistent wealth and success. Rather, the matrix is a map for a journey that can be either circuitous and futile or clear and fruitful. In no event, however, is such a journey easy.

Researchers generate theories and test hypotheses; quite frequently their hypotheses are wrong. Guided by the researcher's maxim that "we learn more from error than from uncertainty," scientists do not despair when a hypothesis is disproved; they rejoice when one more stone is added to the mountain of knowledge required for success. Such intellectual curiosity and learning perspective defines the resilience continuum between learning and leadership. The central lesson of the connection between these two quadrants is not the false hope of avoiding mistakes, but the probable reward of learning from them. The central lesson of the matrix is that we must avoid the search for the perfect leader and focus instead on the search for the leader who consistently occupies the right side of the matrix, the continuum between learning and leadership.

The Journey Between Leadership and Learning

To gain value from the Leadership and Learning Matrix, we must not only label the quadrants but also consider the continua that connect them (Figure 3.2). Because perfection eludes us, the earnest efforts and sincere assurances of strategic planners notwithstanding, it is neither sufficient nor realistic to aspire to the leadership quadrant and regard every other location as a failure. Rather, one must choose the right path to arrive at the leadership quadrant as consistently as possible. The choice of the continuum determines how we use leadership information and whether or not the rest of this book is useful to you.

The Victim Continuum: Blaming Kids, Parents, and the World

Traditional adherents to the business cycle presume that alternation between good and poor results is as inevitable as the rhythms of nature. In an aimless journey that occasionally exchanges good

Figure 3.2. The Leadership and Learning Matrix Continua

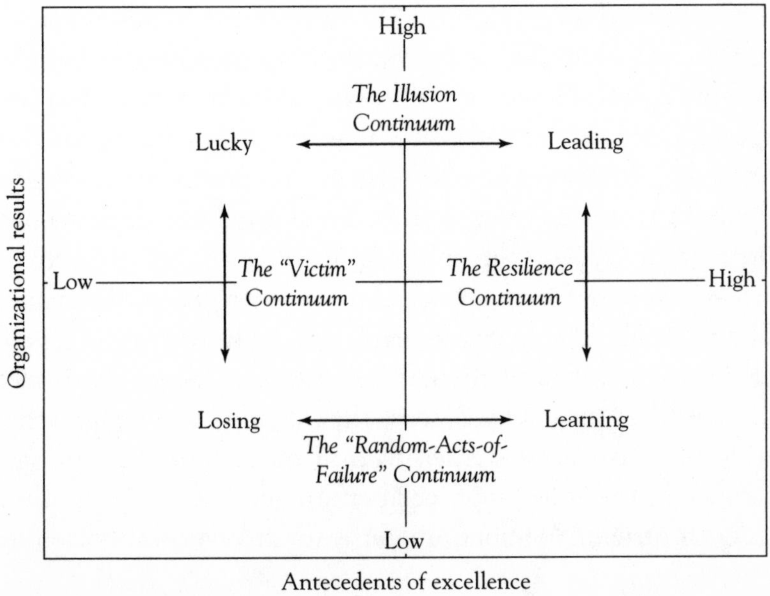

fortune for bad luck (neither related to intended performance), these leaders ride the "victim" continuum, in which success and failure (but especially failure) is the product of external circumstances over which the leader can exercise little control. In education, a similar mood prevails among leaders who are certain that the demographic characteristics of children, the indolence of parents, the opposition of teachers, and the overwhelming demands of the central office all combine to make academic achievement impossible. Although all of these factors are indeed important considerations, the leader riding the victim continuum is paralyzed by externalities. He is frequently depressed, lethargic, angry, and nearly destroyed by stress. If life is so miserable, why does he stay in the game? Because sometimes the results are good. Cynical to the core, he attributes his success to luck, mouthing insincere appreciation and waiting for the next inevitable disaster.

Random Acts of Failure

Some leaders gain a glimpse of understanding of the cause of their poor results, but they fail to apply the lessons they have learned, which leads to an unpleasant journey on the "random-acts-of-failure" continuum. These chronically low performers are found in high-poverty and low-poverty schools, though they tend to congregate in any environment where warm bodies are valued over competent leaders. They survive in an environment of grim despair; a growing national shortage of building administrators allows them to participate in the annual "dance of the lemons" as they are reassigned from one failure to another. One of the greatest failures of public service in general, and public education specifically, is to identify and counsel out of the profession the leaders who ride this continuum. Because they are not learning from their mistakes, each year is another investment in failure rather than a reasoned prospect for improved performance. Worst of all, these leaders contribute to public antipathy toward every school.

The Illusion Continuum: The Golden Touch

Those who believe that one can perpetually ride the "illusion" continuum that connects luck with leadership are also disappointed in the late arrival of the Tooth Fairy. They sustain these aspirations with a facile solution for everything and an attitude that extends beyond optimism, to fantasy. Aspirants to the illusion continuum frequently start in the lucky quadrant and are astonished that the ride is neither consistent nor graceful. There are, in fact, no occupants of this continuum. It is useful only for the recognition that is apparent, not real. Aspiring to it diverts us from our central mission: leadership and learning.

The Resilient Journey of Leadership and Learning

We focus our efforts on the only continuum that offers a high probability of successful leadership: the path that connects learning with leadership. This continuum offers neither perfection nor platitudes, but resilience. Every failure is an investment in learning, provided that the underlying causes are rigorously examined, understood, and applied to future decision making. This continuum is the heart of data-driven decision making and every effective leadership strategy in this book.

Systematic learning from both success and failure is essential for the resilient leader. To ride this continuum, the leader must value honest bad news. Understanding that analysis of teaching, curriculum, and leadership practices requires a range of results that are associated with successful and unsuccessful practices, the resilient leader takes a second look at each apparent student result. She asks, "Is this particular success associated with a measurable improvement in teaching and leadership? If not, how can we possibly sustain it?" In analyzing failure, she asks, "Is this particular failure the result of reduction in our effective practice? If so, that's actually pretty good news, because we know how to fix that. It's the failures we don't understand that we can't fix."

By evaluating leadership and teaching as cause variables, the resilient leader moves away from blame in times of distress and avoids giddiness in times of success. This leader is sustained not by easy victory but by the challenges associated with linking her efforts and those of her colleagues to improved results. She values neither luck nor undefined success, but only those results that she can associate with her own professional effort. This confidence is the heart of resilience. When times are tough, the resilient leader does not rely on platitudes, threats, or fantasy. Rather, she relies on herself and her accumulated wisdom, which links leadership and learning. Only the resilient leader grasps the essential meaning of our next chapter: that leadership makes a difference.

Practical Guidelines for Using the L^2 Matrix

The Leadership and Learning Matrix need not be an abstraction. Leaders can use it successfully if they conduct a self-assessment such as the one in Exhibit 3.1. The essence of this assessment is the answer to two questions. First, "How do I define success?" The quantitative answers to this question, including test scores, student persistence in school, attendance rate, students without disciplinary incident, and so on, represent the vertical axis of the L^2 matrix. The second question is, "What specific professional practices, leadership practices, and curriculum policies did I employ that are associated with these results?" Exhibit 3.2 and Figure 3.3 provide an example of how data can be gathered and displayed.

In Exhibit 3.2, the leader has focused on one variable involving student results, the percentage of students proficient on the state assessment of verbal ability. This is only one illustration of data gathering using the individual teacher as the unit of analysis. In some cases, the variables can be analyzed by building, by groups of students participating in a particular program, or by individual student. The key to identifying the unit of analysis is that the group selected in the effect variable (in this case, the test score) must be the same as the group selected in the cause variable (in this case, the

Exhibit 3.1. Leadership Self-Assessment

Results—Vertical Axis

Student Achievement Result	Number Y-Axis	Data Source

Antecedents of Excellence—Horizontal Axis

Teacher Professional Practices (specify)	Number X-Axis	Data Source

Ordered Pairs for Graph

Line	X-Axis	Y-Axis

frequency of writing performance assessment). Because classroom teachers vary widely with respect to their decisions on writing performance assessment, the classroom teacher was the appropriate unit of analysis in this case.

As Exhibit 3.2 indicates, some teachers assessed students only once a year, while other teachers used semester, quarterly, monthly, or bimonthly assessments. When we combine the information on the top part of Exhibit 3.2 with the information on the bottom part

Exhibit 3.2. Leadership Self-Assessment Illustration

Results—Vertical Axis

Student Achievement Result	Number	Data Source
State test verbal	55	% proficient or higher (Jones)
State test verbal	60	% proficient or higher (Smith)
State test verbal	65	% proficient or higher (Sanders)
State test verbal	70	% proficient or higher (Sackett)
State test verbal	75	% proficient or higher (Cohen)

Antecedents of Excellence—Horizontal Axis

Teacher Professional Practices (specify)	Number	Data Source
Frequency of writing assessment	Annual (1)	Classroom assessment records (Jones)
Frequency of writing assessment	Semester (2)	Classroom assessment records (Smith)
Frequency of writing assessment	Quarterly (4)	Classroom assessment records (Sanders)
Frequency of writing assessment	Monthly (9)	Classroom assessment records (Sackett)
Frequency of writing assessment	Bimonthly (18)	Classroom assessment records (Cohen)

Ordered Pairs for Graph

Line	X-Axis	Y-Axis
Jones	1	55
Smith	2	60
Sanders	4	65
Sackett	9	70
Cohen	18	75

of the chart, we have a set of ordered pairs that can be displayed in Figure 3.3. The leader must note that using a computer is not necessary to perform this analysis. I have worked at teaching and leadership retreats when we used only the blank Exhibit 3.1 to gather data on causes and effects, and then posted the results of the

Figure 3.3. Chart from Exhibit 3.2: Frequency of Writing Assessment and Student Test Results

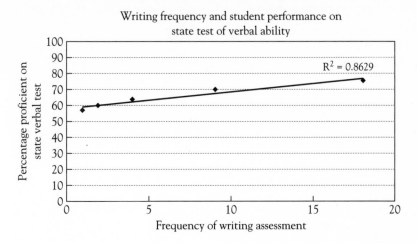

ordered pairs by hand on a wall chart. It is not the elegance of the display that matters nearly as much as the quality of the inference that the teacher or leader can draw from Figure 3.3. In this case, it is clear: the more frequently teachers use writing performance assessment, the higher the percentage of students who are proficient on the state assessment of verbal ability. In fact, the R^2 number near the trend line suggests that about 86 percent of the variation in student test performance is associated with the teaching decisions surrounding the frequency of writing assessment.

How can we ultimately use this information as one piece of the puzzle for the L^2 matrix? The learning leader must understand test scores as well as the extent to which the antecedents of excellence influence them. Therefore, as the L^2 matrix moves from theory to reality, we can create the chart in Figure 3.4. The average test scores from Exhibit 3.2 were not great; an average of only 65 percent of students were proficient or higher. But as Figure 3.3 indicates, this leader knows why some classrooms were proficient and others were not. The understanding of the antecedents of excellence is superior. Therefore, we can begin constructing the L^2 matrix for this leader at the point displayed with an X in Figure 3.4.

Figure 3.4. Sample L² Matrix

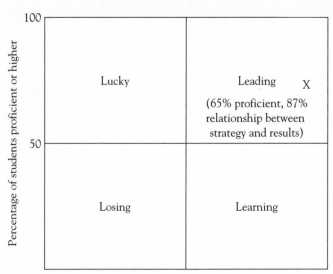

Relationship between strategies and results (R^2)

The first X indicates that this leader's analysis of the frequency of student writing is solidly in the leading quadrant. If the average scores had been lower, but the relationship between writing and student achievement similarly strong, then the X would have been in the learning quadrant. The key to traveling the resilience continuum (see Figure 3.2) is that even when student achievement is down, the leader understands why this is the case.

With every strategy the leader employs, additional Xs can be placed on the L² matrix. Certainly not all of them will appear in the upper-right quadrant. Indeed, some of the most valuable lessons occur from failure, where the vertical axis reveals low student achievement. The difference between those who travel the continuum of resilience and those who are victims, however, is that the learning leader has analyzed the reasons behind failure. This leader continues to test relationships between variables until she finds a high relationship between a cause variable and an effect variable. She relentlessly asks questions until the relationship between strategy and result is revealed.

The victim merely announces results and assumes that demographics are destiny, blaming kids, families, and social conditions; the learning leader asks, "What is the relationship between specific strategies in teaching, leadership, and curriculum and student achievement?" Student achievement results, whether good or bad, do not just happen. They have antecedents. The L^2 matrix reveals whether the leader is finding those antecedents. Only then can we replicate the most effective strategies and discard those that are unrelated to improved achievement.

To apply the L^2 matrix to your own leadership decisions, follow these steps. Reproducible forms to support each of these steps can be found in Appendix A, worksheets A.1 through A.6.

Step one: Identify measures of student achievement. The best way to express these indicators is in the percentage of students proficient or better on a particularly important academic standard.

Step two: Define specific measures of teaching practice, leadership, or curriculum. These indicators can be expressed numerically, such as the frequency of writing assessment, the percentage of assessments using performance assessment, or the number of assignments integrating technology. Once an indicator has been established, record the percentage at each level of performance, such as the percentage of teachers that evidenced distinguished practice, the percentage that were proficient, the percentage that were progressing, and the percentage that were not meeting standards.

Step three: Create ordered pairs using the information in step two, and plot the ordered pairs on a graph. The "cause" variable—the teaching, leadership, or curriculum practice—is listed in the first column and is used to identify the horizontal (X) axis. In the example just introduced, the number of writing assessments yielded the information for this axis. The "effect" variable—the indicator of student achievement—is listed in the second column and is used to identify the vertical (Y) axis. In the example, the percentage of students who were proficient or better produced the information for this axis. Using the ordered pairs, a series of dots can be created similar to the graph in Figure 3.3.

Step four: Determine the relationship between the cause and effect variables (see the sidebars "A Word About Relationships Between Cause Variables and Effect Variables" and "Correlation and Causation"). The easiest way to do this is with a computer spreadsheet program where, with a few simple commands, the user can plot the cause variables in one column, the effect variables in the next column, highlight the two columns, and use the "insert graph" function to create a graph. The "graph trend line" function can then be used to automatically calculate the line of best fit and the regression coefficient associated with that line. It is not necessary for your staff to endure a statistics lesson about regression analysis; common sense suffices. The relationship between the cause variables and effect variables will be clear to the leaders and staff members, and a rational decision can be made to replicate a sound strategy, refine a measurement, or discard a strategy altogether.

Step five: Plot the relationship between cause and effect (the measurement used in the example in Figure 3.4 was R^2, but other measures of association between the cause and effect variable will do) along with the student achievement on your personal Leadership and Learning Matrix. If you had uniformly great student achievement results and every single cause variable that you measured had a high measurable relationship to those results, then every dot on your Leadership and Learning Matrix would be in the upper-right quadrant. In the real world, however, some indicators of achievement are high and some are lower. Sometimes we choose variables that are highly related to student achievement, and sometimes we choose variables that are completely unrelated.

Accumulating marks on your personal matrix tells you not only about the quality of achievement but also about the quality of measurement. Even if you have some instances of low achievement, if the cause variables are highly related to achievement then at least you have a blueprint for action and a deep understanding of how to improve performance in the future. On your personal matrix, the points are arranged on the two right quadrants, and you are traveling the resilience continuum between leadership and learning. In the learning quadrant, you can recognize the value of honest bad news. Student achievement is not at the level you wish, but your leadership is clear and decisive; you can make a positive impact on the future. A leader, however, who is consistently gathering cause indicators that are unrelated to achievement resides on the left-hand side of the matrix. Even with good results, this leader is merely lucky and, with a combination of unintelligible causes and poor results, will join Homer Simpson in the lower-left quadrant.

To apply the lessons of this chapter and create your own Leadership and Learning Matrix, use the forms in Appendix A. Forms A.1 through A.7 take you through the steps necessary to begin your matrix. The forms are reproducible and may be used for professional development activity with your colleagues.

A Word About Relationships Between Cause Variables and Effect Variables

When we look at a graph with points scattered about it, there are typically three types of relationship that might occur (Figure 3.5).

The first one is a positive relationship, such as the chart in Figure 3.3. In general, the points on the graph are arranged from the lower-left quadrant to the upper-right quadrant. In simple terms, we might say that "the more we apply the cause variable, the more we get of the effect

Figure 3.5. Types of Relationship Between Cause Variables and Effect Variables

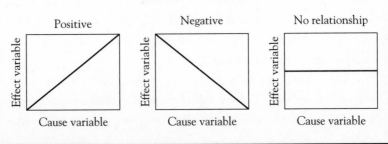

variable." If we measure the slope of the line running from the lower left to the upper right, we find its maximum value is 1.0. Sometimes researchers use the square of the slope of the line to express the amount of variation in the effect variable that is associated with a change in the cause variable.

The second type of relationship is negative. In general, these points are arranged from the upper-left quadrant to the lower-right quadrant. This relationship suggests that "the more we apply the cause variable, the less we get of the effect variable." For example, if the cause variable is the number of absences from school and the effect variable is measured student achievement, we might expect that a greater number of absences is associated with a lower degree of achievement—a negative relationship. The lowest value of the slope of the line running from the upper left to the lower right is -1.0. If we are consistent in our practice, however, and square that number, then a slope that is $-.8$, for example, is the product of $-.8$ and $-.8$, or a positive $.64$. When we record the R^2 value on the L^2 matrix, that is the number we record, because it expresses the degree to which our presumed cause variable is really related to the effect variable we are trying to influence.

Let me emphasize again: it is not necessary to use advanced statistical analysis to complete the Leadership and Learning Matrix. What is absolutely essential, however, is that the leader be willing to analyze systematically both the effect variables—changes in student achievement—and the cause variables—indicators of teaching, leadership, and curriculum. By simply gathering and plotting those numbers, the relationship—or lack of it—to student achievement is evident.

The third type of association between cause and effect variables—and by far the most common one that educational researchers find—is the absence of a relationship. In this relationship, the points are scattered all over the chart with no apparent relationship, and the line of best fit is a horizontal line across the page. It does not appear to make any difference what happens to the cause variable; when it is high, there are both high effects and low effects, and when the cause variable is low, there are again high effects and low effects.

The reason you find cause variables with no relationship to effect is first of all that we are measuring the wrong thing. For example, when we measure technology implementation by variables such as "number of connections to the Internet" or "number of minutes on the computer," we rarely find an association with student achievement. If, by contrast, we find better measures of technology, such as the frequency of revised and edited student work using technology or the frequency of assignments in which the same concept is represented in two or more ways using technology, then we are more likely to find an association to student achievement.

The second reason for the absence of a relationship between the cause and effect variables is that we have identified a cause variable that is truly unrelated to student achievement. This happens frequently in staff development programs when the putative cause variable is the percentage of teachers who have been trained in a particular program, but the training was never related to classroom behavior. Training alone does not influence achievement, and the absence of a correlation tells us to stop wasting money in such a manner.

Correlation and Causation

Because the analysis of this chapter rests upon the relationship between variables that have been labeled "cause" and "effect," it is important to note that there is an important difference between statistical association (or correlation) and causation. Research critics are frequently given to the chant "correlation is not causation"; thus this argument deserves a close look.

First, correlation and causation are not mutually exclusive. In fact, where there is causation, there is certain to be correlation. For example, few would doubt that absence from school is a cause of low achievement; we can consistently plot attendance on the horizontal axis of a graph, plot student achievement on the vertical axis, and find that as attendance increases, so does student achievement. There is both causation and correlation. However, the mere existence of correlation does not automatically imply causation. Only after a series of repeated investigations and studies can researchers conclude, for example, that the association between cigarette smoking and lung cancer is not, as the tobacco lobbyists insisted in the 1950s and 1960s, a mere statistical correlation, but an indication of causation. Similarly, I would recognize that some teaching strategies (such as the frequency of nonfiction writing) may not be a direct causal link to improved student achievement in math, science, and social studies, even though there are consistent correlations between writing and achievement in those subjects.

If we only have correlation without causation, why is the Leadership and Learning Matrix valuable? First, using correlation is helpful for guiding leadership decision making because it helps to test prevailing hypotheses about student achievement. In the case of writing (with, of course, editing, revision, and rewriting), the existence of the correlation to higher student achievement may not prove causation, but it clearly disproves the prevailing allegation by many educators and principals that they "don't have time to do more writing," presumably because such an emphasis on writing would prevent them from adequately covering the curriculum in other subjects, and that would cause scores in those other areas to decline. The existence of a positive relationship between writing and achievement disproves the hypothesis, thus giving leaders a valuable logical tool to undermine the "I don't have the time" arguments that prevail in schools today. Second, the existence of multiple correlations over time allows leaders and researchers to proceed from correlation to causation, just as medical researchers have been able to do. The allegation that correlation is not causation is not a reason to abandon correlation, but rather to understand the limits of this tool, to use it to test hypotheses, and to accumulate information over time to guide and inform effective leadership decision making.

Finally, educational leaders must ask what alternatives are available to them. However frail correlation may be in comparison to the mythical perfection of proven causation, the ideal is not our option. We have correlation, carefully practiced and recorded in this book, or we have speculation, personal preference, whim, and the fad of the month. If I have a professional practice that is consistently associated with improvement in student achievement, I will happily make decisions on the basis of that "mere correlation" rather than the breathless enthusiasm and vague allusions to unspecified research that dominate so many popular educational decisions.

Chapter Four

Leadership Matters

How Leaders Improve the Lives of Students, Staff, and Communities

Leadership Keys

The larger in-box: forces beyond the leader's control

Define what you can influence

Effective feedback for students

Get parents on your side

Collaboration without capitulation: communication with the faculty

Know the consequences of a leadership vacuum

There are two in-boxes on the desk of every educational leader, one of which contains the complaints that demand most of our time and about which one can do very little; the other contains the matters over which one has some influence. In the larger in-box are the myriad factors beyond the control of the leader. Among the litany of complaints in this in-box:

- Children should be better prepared before they come here.
- Teachers should be fully qualified and experienced for the position to which they are assigned.
- Parents should be more supportive.
- Children should receive more rest and better nutrition.
- Central office administrators should be more empathic and less demanding.

- Voters should be more appreciative of the sacrifices of teachers and administrators.
- Legislators should be more sensitive to the needs of public education.
- The Red Sox should win the World Series.

These all have one thing in common: no matter how frequent and passionate our complaints, we can do very little to change them. Don Quixote was a charismatic figure, and tilting at windmills was his specialty. Leading an educational enterprise was not. If we must find a figure from antiquity to emulate, it is neither the idealistic Don Quixote nor the eloquent Demosthenes, who was reportedly so fluent that he could speak with rocks in his mouth. Our aim is not to impress with grandiloquent speech, but to move with passion and meaning. Leaders who want to be effective do not wish merely for their colleagues to feel good but rather to have their colleagues feel that their work matters. Ultimately, it is not self-affirmation that endures; it is a feeling of consequence that lasts. The only reason we can survive the trials of the professional of teaching and educational leadership is that our work matters. We do not end the year saying "I beat the competition by 2 percent" or "The boss liked me" or "I survived the rat race another year." We persevere because we can end the year by saying with conviction:

> We won some and we lost some, but our work made a profound difference in the lives of children. They may not thank us now; in fact, they probably won't. But we know that our work matters, and in time they will know it as well. Even some of my colleagues didn't appreciate my work, but popularity is not the standard here; effectiveness and impact on the lives of kids are all that matters. So I didn't win the Demosthenes oratorical competition. I'm not trying to be Demosthenes. I'm not even trying to be Horace Mann. I'm just trying to be the best teacher and leader I can be.

This sort of self-confidence is unusual, but it is possible if the leader has a clear understanding of the difference between popularity and effectiveness. In the final analysis, a leader does not influence people; nor does the leader influence attitudes and beliefs. The leader can only influence behavior.

Define What You Can Influence

The first and most important influence exerted by a leader is on his or her own behavior. The leader has the most direct impact on the models that he or she establishes in human relationship, time management, professional development, and a host of other areas. The value of leadership modeling far exceeds the impact of memos, seminars, and self-help books. The second greatest influence of the leader is over the behavior of colleagues. Notice that it is not attitudes and beliefs that the leader primarily influences, but behavior. This is counterintuitive for many people in organizations, since the leader seems to devote an extraordinary amount of time to matters of belief and personal attitudes, and this is consistent with conventional wisdom. After all, are not leaders supposed to inspire—or at the very least manipulate, cajole, and influence—their subordinates to act nobly in response to the grand vision of the leader?

Such a vision is appropriate only for those who believe in the Leadership Fairy. That fiction, though quite popular, is available on other shelves at the bookstore. The nostrum that we must first have buy-in, positive attitude, and rock-solid beliefs before behavior change is possible is an hypothesis more distinguished by its popularity than its evidentiary support. In fact, attitude does not precede behavior; behavior precedes attitude. The most important leadership insight is that we are not called to influence beliefs, but to influence behavior. If behavior is successful, belief follows. But no matter how impassioned belief may be on a transitory basis, it does not persist if not accompanied by successful behavior.

Consider the example of diet, exercise, and physical health. Few people enjoy exercise, but many enjoy the results of exercise: the energy, the compliments, the emotional high, and the physical well-being associated with exercise. The first step in creating a successful chain of events is rarely acceptance of an intellectual connection between exercise and health. If that were the case, Twinkies, beer, and corn chips would be absent from supermarket shelves. Instead, we forfeit the snacks and brew and accept the regimen of exercise because our decision makes a difference to something that matters to us. We are not impotent victims of fast food demons.

We demonstrate our power to make a difference not with grandiloquent speeches but with a thousand small decisions that improve our health. At the end of the day, we may not have lost our appetite for junk food, but we can control it because, as a direct result of our behavior, we finally recognize the value of healthy choices. If an educational leader asks teachers to engage in difficult and challenging practices in classroom assessment or professional collaboration, the reaction may range from reluctance to open opposition. Acceptance comes only after successful experience, and that occurs even though some reluctance and opposition continues.

As I was writing this chapter, I was interrupted by a phone call from a woman who began the conversation by saying, "I thought you were crazy and wrong three years ago, but I guess I have to thank you now." Her school had dramatically changed its early literacy practices, including a significant increase in time for literacy and meaningful commitment to more student writing. The move was unpopular, with reactions from cynicism to rage. Three years later, the improvements in student achievement have made the decision, in retrospect, far more popular. But neither the improved performance nor the change in attitude would have come had not the leader of that organization held the courage and wisdom to know that change in behavior precedes change in belief. Had the leader waited for everyone on the staff to buy in and accept the wisdom of the literacy program, their children would still be mired in an environment of poor literacy skills and little hope for the future.

Effective Feedback for Students

If the most important influence leaders have is over their own behavior, what specifically can they do? In the educational setting, the leader cannot take over instruction of every subject in every classroom. Thus many a leader attempts to micromanage the classroom interaction between students and teachers by mandating use of teacher-proof curriculum tools. If every move is scripted, the leader reasons, then the opportunities for human error are reduced and nothing is left to chance. A better strategy is for the leader to identify the interactions that have the most influence on student achievement—the most direct feedback regarding student performance—and participate directly and meaningfully with teachers, students, and parents so that performance feedback is accurate and fair.

The leader cannot direct every classroom interaction, but the ability to influence the report card and other methods of feedback to students is an exceptionally strong means of influencing both student achievement and the professional practice of the teacher. If a leader abdicates this responsibility, evaluation of student work can vary remarkably, with some teachers comparing student work to objective standards while others use the bell curve. Educational leaders cannot claim commitment to academic standards if they do not consistently govern the policies by which student achievement is evaluated. Where the bell curve prevails, standards are a myth. If an A is awarded to the best students regardless of their incompetence, and if less able students receive a poor grade despite their proficiency, then standards have been replaced by the curve. The leader who accepts the frequent claim that grading systems are a matter of academic freedom and must be determined idiosyncratically by each teacher has sacrificed an important influence on professional practice and student achievement.

The leader of a standards-based school makes grading policies clear with these criteria:

• Success is not a mystery. The criterion for success on each assignment, each grading period, and each report card is clear to the teacher, students, and parents in advance. Thus it is possible for all students to receive an A—and possible that no student meets that criterion. The difference is not a matter of the relative performance of the student, but only the result of comparing student performance to a clear and public standard.

• The consequence of failure to meet a standard is not necessarily a low grade, but the opportunity to respect teacher feedback, resubmit student work, and achieve a higher grade. One essential feature of standards is that they evaluate student achievement rather than the speed with which work is completed. Moreover, standards inherently encourage respect for teacher feedback because students always have the opportunity to demonstrate their respect for feedback through improved performance and resubmission of student work.

• Student work is always compared to an objective standard, not to the work of other students.

• The judgment of the teacher is neither mysterious nor isolated, but the transparent result of comparing student work to a scoring guide or rubric based on academic content standards. Teachers who routinely engage in collaborative grading of student work are never faced with the allegation of mystery grading because they and their colleagues have defined precisely and consistently what proficiency means for every assignment in every class.

Get Parents on Your Side

Leadership communication with parents is typically characterized by two qualities: it is late, and it is unhelpful. If the leader communicates only after a failure involving discipline or academic performance, the immediate reaction of parents tends to be punishment or defensiveness, neither of which is particularly helpful. Hence the leader communicates with the threat of consequences for poor results, and the confrontation between leader and parents only escalates to new and unproductive heights. There are far better ways for a leader to communicate with parents proactively and effectively.

Here are some guidelines for the leader of a standards-based school to communicate with parents. Initially, leaders must define academic expectations early, with clarity and precision. Veteran educational leaders follow this advice regularly with regard to discipline. There is normally an absolutely clear set of expectations about drug use, smoking, alcohol abuse, and navel piercing. Ask the same leader, however, if there is an equally clear set of expectations for all students with respect to mathematical proficiency, literacy, and expository writing, and a more equivocal response is sure to follow. Clarity and simplicity are essential here.

In the realm of discipline the effective leader does not post the state criminal statutes on the walls of the school; instead, she identifies a concise list of rules that have meaning and are understood by all students.

In addition, an effective leader does not make vague reference to curriculum documents and hundred-page standards but rather has a clear and easily understood set of academic expectations that all students must achieve. Success, in other words, is not a guessing game, but a matter of following clear and unambiguous instructions.

Collaboration Without Capitulation: Communication with the Faculty

An effective educational leader must not evaluate a teacher's professional practice on the basis of popularity, eloquence, or personal mastery of material. Rather, the evaluation is according to the teacher's response to this question: "What does a student have to know and be able to do to succeed in your class this semester?" If there is a clear, immediate, and coherent response to this question, expressed in language that students and parents can readily comprehend, the leader can enthusiastically validate the professional practices of that teacher. If there is equivocation, ambiguity, hesitancy, or—worst of all—the insinuation that the response to such a question is not the business of an administrator, or the student, or parents, but instead the exclusive province of the teacher, then there is a problem that extends far beyond decorum.

A significant number of teachers and advocates for them sincerely believe that academic freedom means not having to respond to "What must a student do to be successful?" These teachers and advocates, however sincere, are sincerely wrong. A standards-based school is, above all, a place of fairness and transparency. Accepting ambiguity in the name of academic freedom is an unacceptable compromise. Few educational leaders would tolerate ambiguity of expectation from the referee of a high school football game. On the things that we really value, such as the expectation of the quarterback who has the ball on fourth down with three yards to go, educational leaders, policy makers, parents, teachers, and students would never accept a comment such as "That's really none of your concern; I'll judge the quarterback's performance based on my experience and professionalism, and frankly I resent your even asking the question about what's required for a first down—that's a matter for the football teacher to decide." In the context of football, of course, the example is silly. But change the term *football game* to *English literature* and change *fourth down* to *literary analysis* and the example takes on new meaning. The leader in a standards-based environment demands clarity and fairness, and those demands run afoul of the mysterious judgment that has too frequently prevailed in the classroom.

What If You Do Nothing? Consequences of a Leadership Vacuum

There is understandable reluctance among many leaders to make a clear and convincing commitment to standards. On academic matters, the expertise and experience of the individual teacher must be respected, they reason. After all, no school administrator can attain expertise in all academic areas. There is a difference between a leader attempting to define the particulars of academic expectation in every area—an absurd demand for universal expertise—and the more reasonable expectation that the leader specify that academic requirements be clear, precise, and understandable. A principal need not become a curriculum expert in every academic area, but he certainly can picture himself in the place of his students and their parents. From those perspectives, can all parties involved understand what success means? Relying not on personal experience as a parent, teacher, student, or administrator, can they understand what students must know and be able to do to achieve success in a classroom? If the answer is anything other than emphatically affirmative, then standards are an illusion. The leader must build the bridge from chaos to clarity for every stakeholder so that students, teachers, parents, leaders, and the broad community know what success really means.

If leaders fail to insist on standards, they may indulge in the illusion that they are fostering academic freedom. In fact, they have created a vacuum in which fear, suspicion, uncertainty, and guesswork prevail. It is this vacuum that legitimates the vocabulary of students who refer to grades as *given* rather than earned. In the absence of standards-based leadership, students do not know what success means. Parents do not know how to help. Students who begin school with a comparative advantage are inappropriately complacent; students who begin school with a disadvantage are demoralized and unmotivated.

There is a risk in filling this vacuum with a leader's clear and unambiguous expectation for academic standards. First, any change represents risk, because change is uncomfortable. Second, any assertion of leadership authority carries with it the risk of an accusation of authoritarianism, or at the very least loss of popularity for the leader. The leader who equates success with comfort and popularity does not, as a result, succeed in implementing standards. Against these risks, however, the leader must weigh the risk of inaction. What percentage of your students are not proficient now?

What percentage of students are not sufficiently challenged? What percentage of students receive grades that are inconsistent with their level of proficiency or are not related to the academic standards of your state?

These risks represent lifelong consequences for the student, and inevitable consequences for the community and school. In other words, there is no such thing as a risk-free choice. Following the advice of this book and transforming your leadership carries risk; closing the book and doing nothing carries risk. The choice is not to avoid risk, but *to choose* risk wisely and deliberately. By choosing to embrace professional leadership based on academic standards, you accept the risk of unpopularity and discomfort. This choice, however, improves the professional practice of teachers and leaders, instills a higher level of fairness for students, allows a significantly greater number of students to succeed, and challenges those students who are merely competitive without achieving academic standards.

Part Two

Strategic Leadership

Chapter Five

Initiative Fatigue

When Good Intentions Fail

Leadership Keys

Focus: Stop initiative fatigue

Confront the cynics

Principles are more important than programs

Strategic leadership is different from unitary leadership

Values and evidence: a powerful combination

In the New England town where I live, we sometimes have difficulty in distinguishing among buildings that are genuinely historic and those that are merely old. Like a museum without a curator, the area has accumulated buildings since Colonial times, splendidly preserving Abbot Hall and Fort Seawall along with a host of historical buildings, and stolidly protecting other buildings that are old, unsightly, and unsafe. When resources are scarce, as they inevitably are in a governmental budget, the maintenance required for buildings that are merely old robs funds necessary for protecting those that are genuinely historic. Our failure to make wise choices was motivated by our zeal for protecting historical artifacts, but the actual result is the opposite. Our failure to focus, to make difficult and wise choices, to link individual decisions on resources, projects, and tasks—in brief, our failure to exercise strategic leadership—undermines our mission of preserving our heritage for future generations. At every level of decision making, strategic leadership has a pervasive impact, and the failure to implement it properly has grave consequences that threaten the fundamental purpose of an organization.

Educational leaders and policy makers have a similar difficulty as they fail to distinguish between initiatives that represent genuine improvement and those that are merely new. The danger is not in new initiatives, but in the process of accumulation that plagues educational systems. Leaders and organizations demonstrate a resolute unwillingness to evaluate initiatives and discontinue them. The school system has become an organizational pack rat, fearful that if anything is thrown away it might be needed someday. (Actually, the pack rat is not as bad as the unfocused educational system, because your crazy uncle with fifty years of newspapers in the attic does not assign a staff member to read them and report on them regularly.)

The Focus Imperative

The Danger of Leadership Diffusion

I recently visited one of the nation's leading school systems. Student achievement had been historically high, but now progress was stalled. Faculty and administrators were well paid, but relationships between the leadership and teachers were now strained. Facilities that had normally been sparkling were taking on the institutional dullness that comes with slightly less attention to detail than was the case in the past. There was an unmistakable weariness on the faces of staff members, from the newest teacher to the veteran of decades in the system. A new superintendent had recently arrived, brimming with good ideas and new initiatives. Indeed, the administrators seemed to welcome the challenge and the prospects of change, but the stress in the room was palpable.

What was wrong? I had first visited the district fourteen years and three superintendents ago, when a strategic plan with more than 250 action items had just been completed. On the most recent visit, I noticed that the same strategies and action items remained on the plate of the same central office staff, while in the intervening years, each new superintendent had added important and valuable new initiatives.

The Law of Initiative Fatigue states that as fixed resources (time, resources, physical and emotional energy of staff) are divided into a growing number of initiatives, the time allowed for each initiative declines at a constant rate (Figure 5.1), while the effectiveness of each initiative declines exponentially (Figure 5.2). Why does effectiveness decline out of proportion to the restrictions on time and resources? Most initiatives require some minimum amount of resources if they are to be sustained, but there is a more

Figure 5.1. The Cumulative Effect of Unfocused Initiatives on Time and Resources

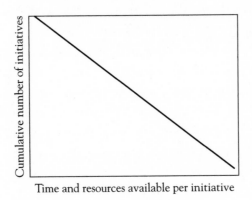

Figure 5.2. The Cumulative Effect of Unfocused Initiatives on Effectiveness

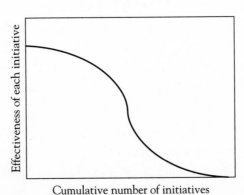

important factor at work. Even the most committed and diligent workers grow weary and cynical when confronted with leadership that does not understand the difference between what is new and what is simply more.

The Keys to Focus: Weed Pulling and Sunsetting

Despite the evident value and promise of each new set of initiatives, the failure of each successive leader to focus the efforts of the system on a few key strategies creates a paradox: the most valuable initiatives receive the least time, energy, and resources. There are only two answers to this dilemma: weed pulling and sun setting.

In the short run, the strategic leader must have a "garden party." Guided by the maxim that one cannot plant flowers without first pulling some weeds, the leader who wishes to avoid the consequences of the Law of Initiative Fatigue is sufficiently disciplined to resist the temptation to announce new initiatives before having reviewed the accumulated baggage of previous decades. The problem, of course, is that one person's weed is another person's prized orchid. The new leader who attempts to engage the process of weed pulling alone will only compound staff morale problems and gain little in the way of new time, energy, and resources to devote to new ideas. There are two corollaries to the Law of Initiative Fatigue:

1. Everyone has weeds. There is not a system, department, office, job description, agenda, or any other element of an educational system that does not have at least a few weeds. As tends to be the case with weeds that have survived over a long period of time, they have deep roots and resist most efforts to pull them.

2. It is much easier and more fun to point out the weeds in other people's gardens than to engage in the unpleasant work of pulling one's own weeds. When the leader proclaims,

"I promise not to start any new initiatives until we have first taken some things off the table," she invariably receives a round of applause. But if she adds, "Everyone will participate in this effort by identifying time-consuming tasks and plans in which you are now engaged that are not contributing to our mission," the crowd grows silent. "But everything I do is important," they claim; "Nothing can be eliminated." Thus do weeds proliferate, choking the life out of the flowers and dominating the resources of the garden.

These corollaries imply that weed pulling must be a collaborative effort, and it must be universally applied. I advise any leader who wishes to have an organizational garden party to begin the process by asking everyone to turn their calendars to a day that has been reserved for a meeting dear to the heart of the leader. The leader then rips that page out of the calendar, deposits it into the ceremonial weed basket, and announces, "You need the time we might have spent at that meeting more than I do, and therefore it is our first weed to be pulled. This meeting is adjourned when everyone has contributed at least one weed to the basket."

The second key to avoiding the consequences of initiative fatigue is to use sunset provisions for all new initiatives. After all, today's flowers can become tomorrow's weeds. The leader must plan now, not as an afterthought, to review every initiative. Most review processes presume continuation of an initiative and consider only how to improve it, but an effective review process begins with the question, "If we were starting to consider this initiative today, would we allocate new time, energy, and resources to support it?" If there is the slightest hesitation to answer in the affirmative, then the leader has a clue that the initiative is supported more by inertia than necessity.

The consequences of the leadership failure to grasp the impact of initiative fatigue are profound. It saps the energy from people and organizations. Worst of all, the leader's toleration of the unfocused accumulation of initiatives feeds into the cynicism and organizational obstructionism that doom even the best of new ideas.

"This Too Shall Pass"

Somewhere in East Africa not long ago, in geological terms, Lucy—our ancestor described, if not discovered by, Professor Leakey—accompanied her son, Grog, to the first school for the emerging species of *Homo sapiens*. The grunts and groans coming from an adjacent cave caught Lucy's attention. They appeared to be coming from the school's faculty lounge; as she drew closer, she heard a flood of complaints. It was, she overheard, something about a new initiative, perhaps something with potential value, such as the wheel or polysyllabic speech. The emphatic grunts and groans made clear, however, that the new idea was unpopular. Lucy heard the unmistakably taciturn voice of Grog's teacher resort to a well-worn quotation from Cro-Magnon ancestors. Roughly translated, the quotation was, "This too shall pass." And so the world's first educational initiative bit the prehistoric dust, and thus began a million years of cynicism and distrust that continues in educational systems to this very day.

Every state in the nation has now adopted educational standards. Iowa, often inaccurately cited as the lone dissenter, requires standards at the local level rather than the state level. Virtually every industrialized nation in the world has established academic standards. Yet on the day that I penned these words, a teacher said, "Go ahead—try to make standards work here—it's just one more fad. This too shall pass."

Call it the "Grog factor." We seem to have inherited a predisposition for cynicism and confidence in failure. The descendants of Grog's teacher, smug in their accusation of the corruption of youth, gave the hemlock to Socrates. They would have carried Galileo to the stake. They doubted the survivability of the anticolonial republic and excoriated both Jeffersonian and Athenian democracies. They found the common schools of New England laughable and were appalled that anyone would dare teach slaves to read. They rejoiced at the concept of "separate but equal" and mourned the clarion call for equity of the *Brown* v. *Topeka Board of Education* decision of the U.S. Supreme Court.

They now rail against the notion that all children can learn and find perverse pleasure in the tribulations of public schools. Although the descendants of Grog's teacher have apprehended multisyllabic speech and comprehended the political landscape of the twenty-first century, little else has changed. Leaders who share a vision for equity and excellence expect to see enthusiasm and goodwill. Instead, they stare into the furrowed brow of the descendant of Grog's teacher.

Strategic Leadership

We think that we have leadership figured out. Certainly, the number of books, journals, and articles devoted to the subject would suggest that many authors believe they have the mystery solved. The number of strikingly different definitions of leadership, all confidently asserted, suggests that as the pile of information grows, our understanding is not necessarily keeping pace.

Leaders and Managers

Many authors have distinguished between the leader and the manager. Kotter (1996) has done the best job, acknowledging the necessity for both leaders and managers and avoiding the simplistic notion that when a manager becomes a little more intelligent, a bit more evolved, or has attended enough conferences on the subject, he is transformed into a leader. Rather, Kotter notes a clear functional difference between the two. The job of management is complex, maintaining the interrelationships between people, technology, and organizational units. Leadership, by contrast, "defines what the future should look like, aligns people with that vision, and inspires them to make it happen despite the obstacles" (p. 25).

Although this distinction between leadership and management is critical, it is not sufficient to distinguish among the types of leaders at the helm of complex organizations, including school systems. Because each school is itself a complex system, there is a difference between a leader who sets the vision for a single system and the leader who deals with the exponentially more challenging task of a system of systems.

Strategic Leaders and Unitary Leaders

The essential need for a leader does not reduce the value and importance of the manager. Similarly, the essential need for strategic leaders does not reduce the need for unitary leaders, the people who lead the faculty through the complex challenges of school reform and myriad change initiatives. The unitary leaders inspire, cajole, demand, and coerce, all within a framework of values and principles that, in the educational context, focus on excellence and equity (Reeves, 2000a). The unitary leader is the foundation of any effective educational system. The great strategic leader is a visionary blowhard if he has not developed a cadre of unitary leaders who make change happen at each school, department, and entity within the system. Great unitary leaders are frustrated change agents caught in a bureaucratic miasma if they are not supported by strategic leaders who allocate time, energy, resources, and emotion among competing systems. Table 5.1 summarizes the characteristics of strategic and unitary leaders.

The distinctions between strategic and unitary leaders are not obvious, because once the appellation of "leader" has been assigned to an individual there is an impulse to presume the almost mystical powers that every leader must have. In fact, there are clear distinctions among leaders. As Table 5.1 indicates, each leadership dimension—implementation, sustainability, and leverage—is quite dependent on whether the leader is unitary or strategic. Whereas the unitary leader depends upon compliance with policies and procedures for implementation, the strategic leader

Table 5.1. Strategic and Unitary Leaders

Leadership Dimension	Strategic Leader	Unitary Leader
Structure	Networks	Hierarchy
Relationships	Agreement, voluntary control	Required compliance with policies and procedures
Implementation leverage	Influence, compelling vision	If vision does not work, then compulsion
Force of sustainability	Ideas more important than individual	Personal charisma of leader

appears far less potent, relying on a network among peers in which voluntary compliance, negotiation, and agreement are the hallmarks. Tim Murphy (personal communication, Mar. 5, 2002) of the Los Angeles County Office of Education is such a strategic leader. Although he can bring the force of law and the threat of reduced funding to the table, he understands that strategic leadership in one of the largest and most complex educational systems in the world relies less upon his threats than upon his network of voluntary compliance. He confesses his frustration over having to persuade schools to send the right people to the right meeting, but he acknowledges that reliance on intimidation and compliance would be a Pyrrhic victory. The persuasive power of "What's in it for me" beats "You have to do it, or else" any day.

The leverage of the strategic leader depends upon a compelling vision, not a definition of success that is associated with compliance. The Rev. Dr. Martin Luther King, Jr., did not cite *Brown v. Board of Education of Topeka, Kansas* nor the numerous court opinions and administrative regulations that were the sequelae of that seminal decision. He did not recite the words, "I have a dream that every employee will comply with section 102.9 of the Board of Education Code of Conduct." Rather, he articulated the dream in which "my four little children will one day live in a nation where they will not be judged by the color of their skin but by the content of their character" (King, quoted in 1996). With a sufficiently compelling vision, the strategic leader needs no threats. It is obvious that the alternative to the vision is unacceptable. This is the reason that a poorly articulated vision statement is worse than no vision at all. The vision of a committee is too long, too complex, and too unfocused to be compelling. Kotter (1996) warns, "Whenever you cannot describe the vision driving a change initiative in five minutes or less and get a reaction that signifies both understanding and interest, you are in for trouble (p. 9)."

The third essential difference between the strategic and unitary leader involves personal charisma. Despite the plethora of "CEO as God" literature, the evidence (Sergiovanni, 2000) suggests that the personal charisma of the leader is not necessarily linked to successful change initiatives. In fact, for long-term sustainability, the strategic leader must acknowledge that ideas are more important than personalities. This ability to subordinate one's ego to ideas that transcend personality is rare. Consider the challenges faced by Elizabeth Smith, a fictional representative of many authentic cases. She is a charismatic leader who would much prefer the implementation and eternal memory of the "Smith Plan" than the depersonalized "Learning for All" plan. Moreover, she has experienced the power of personal charisma when, as a unitary leader, faculty members said, "Liz, I'll do this for you—I sure as heck wouldn't do it for anyone else." Although she takes pride in such a statement, her acceptance of it is evidence that her personal charisma is more powerful than the idea itself. More important, she is acknowledging that the success of this initiative is only as long-lived as her persistence in her present position. Growing tired of the fray, she intends to move soon; every "Smith initiative" will perish the instant she vacates her office.

Thus there is not a hierarchy of personal power and individual charisma as one proceeds from unitary to strategic leader. The successful strategic leader may not be possessed of compelling oratorical skills, nor have the gift of personal persuasion to move the intractable faculty member from recalcitrance to acceptance. The strategic leader may not have the drill sergeant skills to gain compliance through threats and intimidation. The strategic leader may lack the skill to articulate the policies and procedures that implement a vision. But the strategic leader can build a coalition, gain voluntary acceptance of a complex and challenging plan, and create a vision that is more compelling than her own personality.

Leading with Values: The Link Between Standards and Fairness

The Value Imperative

What allows strategic leaders to subordinate their own ego and implement their vision with success? The answer lies with values, and the relationship of those values to specific educational models. Questions of value transcend policies, procedures, and rules. The most disparate elements of the community can agree on principles and values such as fairness, equity, and understanding. These values create a filter by which policies and procedures can be subsequently evaluated. The unitary leader needs policies and procedures, since they create order out of chaos. The strategic leader depends upon principles and values, since they create context for every leadership decision within the system.

Leadership with Values: A Practical Application to Student Achievement

When I ask an audience of a thousand educators and leaders to consider what they would do in the absence of educational standards, I have yet to hear as a response "We would stop teaching reading" or "We would no longer care about poor children." Rather, the audience members uniformly insist that, even without state-imposed standards, they would create classrooms that exemplify rigor, reasoning, thinking, fairness, communications, and intellectual challenge. When I ask, "Why don't you create such a classroom now?" the inevitable response is, "We don't have the time."

This always strikes me as a curious statement, since the clocks in Boston, Paris, Topeka, Beijing, Nairobi, and Peoria all bear a striking similarity to one another. Thus the statement "I don't have the time" must be fundamentally false, as the quantity of available time is the same throughout the globe. The statement "I don't have the time" is, in fact, code for "I fear that if I spend my time differently and pursue my value of rigor, reasoning, thinking, fairness, and intellectual challenge, then I will not be able to cover the curriculum and my students' test scores will decline." Now we have a testable hypothesis. Whereas "I don't have the time" is demonstrably false on its face, the contention that "If I do more good teaching [reasoning, writing, and rigor], my test scores will decline," is subject to an evidentiary test.

Why is an evidentiary test important? Because values—particularly the values related to educational leadership and student achievement—do not exist in a vacuum. Although the values of thinking, reasoning, and writing as the right thing to do are widely accepted, they are rarely practiced. Hypotheses such as "I don't have the time" are also widely accepted, even though they are rarely tested. The strategic leader must not only articulate values but must also eliminate the obstacles that prevent those values from becoming translated into action. In this example, the leader who believes that thinking, analysis, reasoning, and writing are essential for student success must articulate the hypothesis that is the obstacle and then test that hypothesis.

Figure 5.3 expresses this hypothesis, while Figures 5.4, 5.5, and 5.6 test it. In Figure 5.3, the horizontal axis measures the time devoted to writing assessment and the vertical axis represents student achievement results. If the "I don't have the time" hypothesis is true, then the more time is devoted to writing (and consequently the less time is available to cover every element of the curriculum) the lower student achievement scores will be. Hence, the line on the graph extends from the upper left to the lower right. As more time is devoted to writing, scores decline.

Figure 5.3. The "I Don't Have the Time" Hypothesis

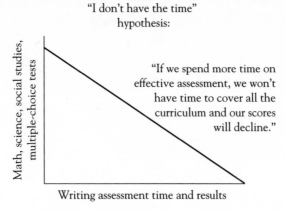

"I don't have the time" hypothesis:

"If we spend more time on effective assessment, we won't have time to cover all the curriculum and our scores will decline."

Source: Center for Performance Assessment.

Figure 5.4. Testing the "I Don't Have the Time" Hypothesis

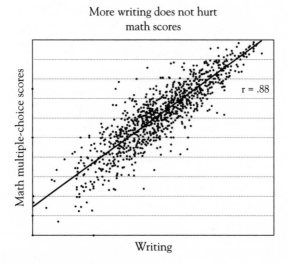

More writing does not hurt math scores

$r = .88$

Source: Center for Performance Assessment.

Figure 5.4 represents one test of the hypothesis. This is actually a synthesis of several observations of the relationship between writing and student achievement. In some cases, the emphasis on writing is measured by the frequency of writing in the classroom, while in other cases the frequency of classroom writing assessment

Figure 5.5. Testing the "I Don't Have the Time" Hypothesis with Social Studies Achievement

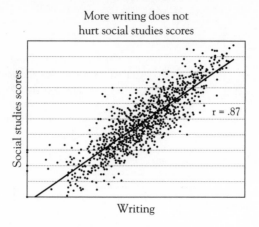

More writing does not
hurt social studies scores

Social studies scores

r = .87

Writing

Source: Center for Performance Assessment.

Figure 5.6. Testing the "I Don't Have the Time" Hypothesis with Science Scores

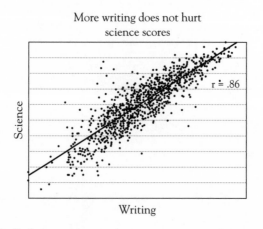

More writing does not hurt
science scores

Science

r ≐ .86

Writing

Source: Center for Performance Assessment.

has been measured. In still other cases, student performance on writing tests has been used to measure the horizontal axis. No matter how the writing variable has been measured—writing time, assessment time, or student writing proficiency—the results are the same, as reflected in Figures 5.4, 5.5, and 5.6. As the emphasis on classroom writing grows, student achievement improves. The line on the graph extends from the lower left to the upper right, indicating that the actual relationship between writing and student achievement is the opposite of that predicted by the "I don't have the time" hypothesis. These findings have also been confirmed in several case studies as well as quantitative analyses (Reeves, 2000c). Figure 5.4 indicates the relationship between an increased emphasis on writing and improved math scores. Figure 5.5 indicates the relationship between an increased emphasis on writing and improved social studies scores. Figure 5.6 indicates the relationship between an increased emphasis on writing and improved science scores. The relationship between writing and achievement has been extensively documented by other researchers as well (Klentschy, Garrison, and Amaral, 2000; Darling-Hammond, 1997; Calkins, 1994).

Values are not outside the realm of evidence. Actually, the value is supported by the evidence.

The notion that because values are transcendent evidence is irrelevant is defensive sophistry. In fact, it is because values are transcendent that the evidence is so important. A challenge to values cannot be resolved by a petulant "'tis-'tain't" controversy. A challenge to values is sustained or defeated by evidence. It was not Galileo's confidence in his understanding of planetary rotation, nor Rome's confidence in Aristotelian formulations of the positions of the heavens, that ultimately resolved the question of the position of the earth and sun. Observation and evidence, painstakingly acquired and meticulously reported, resolved the issue. It is worthy of note that the same Galileo who is remembered for his defense of the position of the sun as the center of our solar system and his courageous advocacy of his position was, using the same intellect and rigorous methods, spectacularly wrong in his analysis of ocean tides.

Hubris, confidence, and rhetoric do not defend values. Evidence defends or undermines values. Strategic leaders do not divine values from mysterious forces; they discern values on the basis of the intersection of principles and evidence. In the context of educational standards, the principle is that rigor, analysis, thinking, reasoning, and communications—most particularly, student writing—is a proper way to educate children even in the absence of standards and testing. These same characteristics that the principled educator pursues in the absence of standards are also related to improved student achievement in an environment in which high-stakes testing and rigorous standards are imposed.

To bring together these disparate and complex ideas, we can consider these conclusions. First, the value of educational standards lies not in the power of a district, state, or federal mandate but in the simultaneous power of the evidence and the value that the teaching and leadership strategies are more important than demographic characteristics in influencing student achievement (Haycock, 1998, 2002; Haycock and others, 1999; Schmoker, 2001; Reeves, 2000a, 2000c). Second, the sustainability of good educational practice, including rigor, thinking, analysis, reasoning, and writing, depends not upon a policy mandate but upon the strategic leader who understands that these strategies should be voluntarily embraced even in the absence of standards. Third, regression coefficients do not respect charisma. Theodore Roosevelt, Ronald Reagan, and Attila the Hun could articulate values unsupported by the evidence, while Mother Theresa, Calvin Coolidge, and Moses (none of whom were known for compelling rhetoric) were able to articulate values that were unpopular but nevertheless true. The strategic leader depends upon neither personal charisma nor transient popularity, but rather upon the confluence of evidence, values, and commitment. The remainder of this book is devoted to applying this iconoclastic model of strategic leadership to the challenges of education.

Leadership Reflections

1. Identify the hierarchy within which you operate. To whom do you report? Who reports to you?

2. Identify the networks *outside* of this hierarchy. List the networks that you have used to get information and make decisions within the past year.

3. How would you compare the impact of the nonhierarchical networks to the formal hierarchical ones? Where do you spend more time? Where do you have the greater impact? What inference do you draw from these observations about future strategic leadership decision making?

4. Think of an instance in which you recently met resistance to a decision that you made and you ultimately overcame that resistance. Describe the situation in as much detail as you can recall. What was the key to your overcoming resistance: compliance with a mandate, acceptance of a compelling vision, or another factor?

5. What are the "big ideas" associated with the senior leadership of your organization? List them; describe three of them so that someone unfamiliar with your organization would understand what they mean. Which of these big ideas can be sustained without the leaders that you now have in place? What inference do you draw from that?

Chapter Six

Saving Strategic Planning from Strategic Plans

Leadership Keys

The limits of strategic planning

The limits of vision and mission

The limits of comprehensive reform

Beyond the limits: a new vision of strategic
leadership

If the success of educational leadership depended upon the girth of documents, the quantity of initiatives, the loftiness of the rhetoric, or the complexity of the plans, then surely every student and teacher would be successful. Schools are straining under the weight of initiative fatigue, while administrators add additional programs to fix educational problems but routinely fail to remove previously established initiatives. The result is inevitable, with a fixed amount of time spread over a growing number of programs. Superficiality replaces focus and frustration displaces effectiveness. In this chapter, we explore the three dominant themes of educational reform in the past two decades: strategic planning, vision and mission statements, and comprehensive reform models. Identifying flaws in these themes does not necessarily imply that they should be abandoned, but they must be seriously reexamined. Strategic leadership calls for choices. Most important, leaders must choose what *not* to do (Collins, 2001).

Saving Strategic Planning from Strategic Plans

The divergence of opinion on the value of strategic planning could hardly be more dramatic. The advocates of strategic planning, including the legion of consultants who produce imposing documents, note plausibly that an organization requires a clear link among mission, vision, values, strategies, and tasks. Documentation of this process, they argue, is not the detritus of consultants gone stark-raving mad, but merely the necessary road map for success. On the other end of the continuum of opinion, we find a Harvard Business School professor, who notes with typical academic restraint: "If the goal is to create new strategies, you might as well dance naked round a campfire as go to one more semi-sacramental planning meeting. No wonder that in many organizations, the whole notion of strategic planning has been devalued. How often has it produced any radical value-creating insights?" (Hamel, 2000, p. 21). Many educational leaders share Hamel's skepticism about the strategic planning process, with one leader saying bluntly that after seventeen years at the helm of the nation's leading professional development organization, he had not seen strategic planning yield its planned results (Dennis Sparks, personal interview, Mar. 24, 2002).

It is not that strategic planning is without value; it is essential for any effective organization. In fact, strategic planning is so important that it should not be left exclusively in the hands of strategic planners; nor should the evidence of strategic planning be restricted to production of a strategic plan. The document itself does not fully reflect the value of the process; that lies in the communication, the linkages, and the focus provided by the process of collaborative data analysis and goal setting (Stan Scheer, personal interview, Mar. 13, 2002). Most strategic planning processes, says Sparks, confirm existing mental models by starting with a statement of belief systems that yield some typically expected statement, such as "All children can learn," sometimes boldly modified to be "All children will learn," or "All children will learn at a high level." The missing conversation, however, is the confrontation of the chasm between these statements and the reality of schools, policies, curricula, and other operational evidence of belief systems. The process of articulating values and belief systems is one thing; the process of listing the values and beliefs that are reflected in the daily lives of schools is quite another. Unless we are willing to say that beliefs have fundamentally changed, then we should not expect strategic planning, no matter how elaborate the process, how large the document, or how pretentious the vocabulary, to yield meaningful improvement.

Strategy does have value, but only when it is the work of senior leadership. The leader who regards himself as a big-picture thinker delegating the details to someone with appropriate technical skills is missing an opportunity if he does not take personal responsibility for development, consideration, and acceptance or rejection of strategy. The trouble with publishing a document with an imposing title and lots of group buy-in is that some of the strategies are just plain bad. Others are beyond the resources of the school system. Still others are fine ideas but divert focus from the central challenge faced by the school system and the primary mission the leader is attempting to achieve. Planners are rarely congratulated for producing a document that is elegant, focused, and brief. I have witnessed grant providers and school leaders alike complain about the brevity of a document, not recalling that three hundred pages of tripe a year earlier was hardly the recipe for success. If the leader were responsible for writing and reviewing strategic plans, they would be far shorter and more focused on the most important challenges facing the school system. This is not the fault of the planners, as they lack the wide perspective and deep understanding of the need for focus possessed by the senior leader. As Hamel notes, "Giving planners responsibility for creating strategy is like asking a bricklayer to create Michelangelo's *Pieta*" (2000, p. 20). Effective plans do not fill the Uffizi gallery, but rather represent one compelling vision. The leader must listen to a variety of points of view in creating the plan; however, choices must be made on the basis not of popularity but of evidence. When facilitators engage in the exercise of setting priorities by asking many participants to place a certain color of dotted adhesive paper next to a proposition of fact, their process may have names that suggest sophistication, but this is no more than sophistry. A process that allows group opinion to substitute for data may be popular, but it certainly is not strategic.

What Is "Strategic," Anyway?

The operational definitions of the words *strategy* and *strategic* are confusing and inconsistent. The root of the terms comes from the Greek word *stratos*, which refers to a military camp, and its Latin counterpart *stratus*, referring to things that are spread out. The dictionary definition primarily refers to military activity. The secondary definition of strategy in *Merriam Webster's Collegiate Dictionary* (tenth edition) is "a careful plan or method: a clever stratagem" and "the art of devising or employing plans or stratagems toward a goal." Is *stratagem* just another word for strategy? Let us hope not, as the same dictionary says that a stratagem is "an artifice or trick in war for deceiving and outwitting the enemy" and "a cleverly contrived trick or scheme for gaining an end." These implications for strategic planning might help to explain the cynicism and doubt that surrounds the entire subject. The definition used by one prominent consulting firm illustrates the point: "Strategic Planning is the means by which a community of people create artifactual [sic] systems to serve extraordinary purpose. Strategic Action defines the three kinds of action and explains how each can be instrumental in realizing the plan in two ways: by conforming organization to action and by systemizing all action. The result is that organizations can go far beyond merely improving that which already exists. They can actually create new systems that are capable of constant emergence—always vital, always creative" (Cambridge Group, 2002).

The business perspective on strategic planning is a bit less obscure and flamboyant. Robert Kaplan, of the Harvard Business School, refers to strategies as "unique and sustainable ways by which organizations create value" (Kaplan and Norton, 2001, p. 2).

Ulrich, Zenger, and Smallwood claim that strategy "establishes the boundaries for desired results" (1999, p. 35). One of the clearest contributions to strategic planning literature comes from the Internet Nonprofit Center, a project of the Evergreen State Society in Seattle. For this organization, strategic planning is "a disciplined effort to produce fundamental decisions and actions that shape and guide what an organization is, what it does, and why it does it, with a focus on the future" (Internet Nonprofit Center, 2002). Wisely, the authors of this definition take pains to identify not only what strategic planning is but what it is not. They explain that strategic planning "is not a substitute for the exercise of judgment by leadership. . . . Just as the hammer does not create the bookshelf, so the data analysis and decision-making tools of strategic planning do not make the organization work—they can only support the intuition, reasoning skills, and judgment that people bring to their organization" (Internet Nonprofit Center, 2002).

Clarity in Strategic Planning

Given how unhelpful dictionary definitions and the inconsistency of the terminology currently in use are, we must bring some clarity to the topic by first clarifying the definition of terms. For the purposes of this book, we employ these definitions:

- *Strategy:* a description of decisions linked to the mission, information, and results.
- *Strategic leadership:* the simultaneous acts of executing, evaluating, and reformulating strategies, and focusing organizational energy and resources on the most effective strategies.

We return to these definitions throughout the following chapters. Their simplicity is important because of what the definitions omit. Strategy is not attitude, cultural value, or program. Strategy is a decision and it is as good or as bad as the mission and information to which it is linked. Strategic leadership is not a grand vision by a deep thinker in a three-piece suit striding about the bridge of the metaphorical battleship yelling orders. Strategic leadership involves the acts of many team members who not only execute plans well but have the organizational and emotional support necessary to challenge one another and themselves as they evaluate and reformulate their strategies. If someone in your organization has not challenged the chief executive in the past few months, then it is unlikely that strategic leadership is taking place. If senior leaders in your organization do not systematically challenge themselves and their assumptions, then the preconditions for strategic leadership are absent.

Effective Strategy Without a Strategic Plan

One complexity surrounding the topic of successful strategic leadership is that so many of the activities and documents that bear the label "strategic" are not really helpful. It is certainly possible to be a successful strategic leader without engaging in a labyrinthine process frequently associated with strategic planning and without creating a document called the "strategic plan." One can also be a woefully ineffective strategic leader while straining under the weight of an enormous and complex strategic plan. My purpose is not to condemn the strategic planning process, but rather to distinguish between models that have been effective and those that have merely generated pain, perplexity, and paper.

The most commonly used strategic planning models proceed from the vision, mission, and values of the organization to analysis of needs, to developing strategies to meet those needs, and to creating action plans for each strategy (Figure 6.1). Most planning models involve a large number of stakeholders: board members, community leaders, teachers, parents, administrators, students, senior citizens, and a variety of other interest groups. The theory behind such widespread participation is that it yields equally widespread support for the plan and shared understanding of the challenges of the organization. Observations and interviews with people involved in the strategic planning process reveal potential

Figure 6.1. Traditional Strategic Planning Model

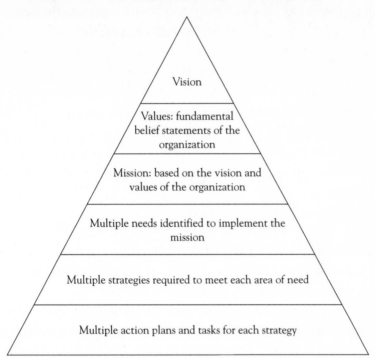

for clarity and cohesiveness as well as the potential for chaos and exhaustion.

Few leaders would argue with the ideal strategic plan. Action steps are linked to the mission. The mission leads to action steps. Work and investment of resources is therefore automatically relevant and the vision is thus transformed into action. This ideal, however, is elusive in practice. Although there are many types of strategic planning model, including those facilitated externally by experts and those created internally by the staff of a school system, all the plans I have examined have one characteristic in common: they are very, very large. Dozens of strategies and hundreds of action plans result, particularly when the process itself rewards accumulation, detail, and specificity. When I ask leaders who have been responsible for creating a strategic plan if they can recall a single strategy created in the process that was later withdrawn by design, they are silent. They can think of many strategies and action steps that were discarded from neglect and many that were dropped by default because the partisans who created the plan did not participate in implementing it. But selecting the "not to do" list by default and neglect can hardly be called strategic. Former President Dwight Eisenhower, the Supreme Allied Commander in World War II and clearly a believer in strategic planning, warned that we should "rely on planning, but don't trust plans" (Gary, 2002, p. 7).

Mission and Vision with Meaning

Some mission statements and accompanying visions are clear. For example, the mission of the Littleton Public Schools is "to educate students for the future by challenging every individual to continuously learn, achieve, and act with purpose and compassion." The vision statement of the same district is "Exceptional community, extraordinary learning, expanded opportunity, and success for all students" (Stan Scheer, personal interview, Mar. 13, 2002). The mission of the Norfolk (Virginia) public schools is simply that "All students will learn and succeed, and all means all." The Cleveland Heights—University Heights school district is a bit less succinct, but still focused and clear. Its mission reads: "Our schools exist to provide students with an excellent education that prepares them for life as engaged and productive citizens. We accomplish this mission by offering a wide array of educational, social, and cultural opportunities and by cultivating strong partnerships with families and community." Buhler, Kansas, takes the prize for brevity with a mission that says, "In a safe and caring environment, we offer equitable education opportunities so that each student can excel."

Mission Out of Control

Unfortunately, a number of other mission and vision statements are the rhetorical equivalent of the horse assembled by a committee that resulted in a camel. These mission statements are ponderous and pretentious, incorporating every bit of jargon of the moment, assiduously including every idea and concept, and earnestly attempting to make every single person on the committee feel valued. Imagine:

> As our students prepare to enter the global village, the parents, teachers, board members, students, and citizens of Pleasant Valley will empower every child to engage in lifelong learning and success, utilizing rigorous curriculum that individually meets the needs of our diverse student body, providing multiple assessments, and delivering a curriculum that prepares students for the twenty-first century while it is cognizant of their diversified needs. In addition, we will instill the values of our community that include a respect for differences, a commitment to fairness for all stakeholders in the educational enterprise, shared decision making, strong parental and community voices, respect for the differently abled, and a commitment to a multi-cultural perspective in all that we do.

I could go on, but it is too painful. When Scott Adams's cartoon character Dilbert emerges from his cubicle to make trenchant observations on the frivolity of some organizational fad, he lumps together many such efforts with the term "process pride."

From Divergence to Convergence

There is an inherent tension between the need of the leader to be open-minded to a variety of points of view and the need for focus. Paul Houston, executive director of the American Association of School Administrators and one of the leading voices in America and abroad for system-level improvement, describes this challenge as the transition the leader must make from divergence to convergence in any planning process. At the beginning of the process, Houston explains, a variety of views are essential and the leader must tolerate some contention, ambiguity, and divergence. If this unwieldy process continues unabated, however, then chaos reigns. The leader must make a gradual but definitive turn toward convergence, in which tough choices are made and the unmistakable but unpopular truth is spoken that not every idea in the brainstorming process is equally good. Leaders who fail to make this transition doom their systems and their colleagues to initiative fatigue (personal interview, Mar. 28, 2002).

Criteria for an Effective Mission Statement

A mission statement has the potential to help an organization gain focus and clarity, filtering out legions of extraneous initiatives with the simple question, "Is this consistent with our mission?" Moreover, an effective mission statement allows every person involved with an organization to understand what it is about and make a conscious decision as to whether the mission is sufficiently engaging and compelling to warrant an investment of emotional and intellectual energy. In schools, the physical participation of some participants, such as students, is involuntary. The same is essentially true of long-term employees, who have no financial and occupational alternatives other than continued employment. Physical participation can be compulsory, but the engagement of emotion and intellect on which every successful organization depends is completely voluntary. One thing that businesses, nonprofit organizations, and school systems all share is this truth: paychecks do not engage emotions. The leader depends on the hearts and minds, not merely the hands and seats, of employees, and thus a mission statement is at the heart of this fundamental organizational need.

The Value of Brevity. An effective mission statement shares two criteria: it is brief and it is passionate. A great mission statement is no longer than a single sentence. It should fit on a business card and be something that is easy for your newest employee to memorize. At the Center for Performance Assessment, our mission is on everyone's business card, from the newest administrative assistant to the chairman of the board. It says simply, "Improving student achievement through standards, assessment, and accountability." Each year there is the temptation to become involved in some other service or product, and we ask ourselves two simple questions: Will it improve student achievement? Does it fit into standards, assessment, and accountability? This saves a great deal of time, energy, and money. I wonder how many hours of school board meetings and superintendent's cabinet meetings would be saved if there on the top of every page of the agenda was the question, "Will it improve student achievement?"

For almost ten years, we have focused on standards, assessment, and accountability. There are many other areas where we might have some interest and at least a thousand fads and whims that decorate the catalogues of conferences and staff development programs, but we remain focused on improving student achievement through standards, assessment, and accountability. A school system sometimes has duties forced on it by governmental entity or population shift, and so a mission to educate children falls under the broader framework of giving students food, shelter, and survival skills in a new country (all essential to success in education). If the mission statement remains relentlessly focused, every bus driver, cafeteria worker, computer programmer, administrative assistant, teacher, aide, leader, student, and board member knows how his or her daily decisions relate to the mission. If a mission statement attempts to respond to trends rather than lead them, then focus is abandoned and the personal decisions of the stakeholders bear little relationship to a mission, because they rarely know, understand, or care what that mission is.

The Essence of Passion. Second, an effective mission statement is compelling. It engages the emotions of people. Student achievement is one of those things, in Michael Fullan's turn of phrase, that are "worth fighting for" (Fullan and Hargreaves, 1996). The same is true of standards and good accountability systems, which are essential to achieving the fundamental human values of fairness and equity (Reeves, 2002b). Contemplation of compelling emotions may appear to be so personal and private that some leaders are reluctant to approach the issue. After all, they reason, personal emotional responses are culturally based and psychologically influenced. Why should the leader presume to enter into such delicate territory? Why indeed. This is the central challenge of leadership, and the leader who fails to recognize her role in the emotional engagement of the people with whom she shares her professional life is accepting the life of a bureaucrat. She may aspire to manage processes and paper, but she will not lead people.

Richard Boyatzis, Annie McKee, and Daniel Goleman (2002) persuasively argue that the events of September 11, 2001, give a special urgency to the need for the leader to consider the issues of emotional engagement and passion. They suggest that individuals who were in the buildings under attack as well as those who watched the horrific events on television will have in the months and years ahead the opportunity to redefine their principles and reconsider their future. For some people, this process implies a significant revision of their behavior, occupation, and lifestyle. For most people, however, it involves finding greater meaning in what they are doing now. Thus the mission statement of an educational system must open the door to reconsideration of these questions: "What am I doing here?" "Why does my job matter?" "If I were starting life again today, would I want to sign up for this mission?"

A mission statement that is long on process and jargon and short on emotional engagement never produces satisfactory answers to these questions. A mission statement that can be recited like a morning meditation, with calm determination and total clarity, is essential. John Kotter (2002), one of the world's leading experts on the leadership of change, notes that despite the business professor's preference for quantitative analysis, he is developing a "great appreciation of the limits of the analytical—and of the importance of showing people by example and touching their emotions." He continues: "Both thinking and feeling are essential, both are found in successful organizations, but the heart of change is in our emotions. The flow of see-feel-change is more powerful than [that] of analysis-think-change."

Is your mission statement brief and passionate? You don't need a strategic planning consultant to answer the question. You already know the answer to the first part; you can ask a half-dozen colleagues about their level of passion to quickly find the answer to the second part.

Reforming Comprehensive School Reform

"Just tell us what to do," the exasperated leader demands, "and we'll do it." Many vendors offered a ready reply, at a cost, to that request under the mantle of whole school reform. Many millions of dollars later, the shakeout is just beginning. Some school districts, such as Memphis, Tennessee, have performed a complete about-face, changing from commitment to engaging a whole-school reform model in every school in the district to complete abandonment of the project. The frustration of school leaders with these models is understandable; the RAND Corporation reported that more than half of the more than two hundred programs that researchers studied had shown no improvement in student achievement relative to comparable schools without the reform models in operation (Viadero, 2001). With the budget for whole-school reform models increasing to more than $300 million and now becoming a permanent part of federal educational legislation, this strategy deserves close examination (Sack, 2002).

The Context of Reform Models

When I taught doctoral-level research classes, I would ask my students to bear in mind two important principles. First, life is multivariate; beware of any assertion that X is the exclusive cause of Y. Second, not everything can be measured with a number; wise researchers look at quantitative data through a qualitative lens. Examining the research on comprehensive school reform models is testimony to the truth of these fundamental research principles. In a comprehensive evaluation of school reform models, the RAND Corporation (2001) announced these not-terribly-surprising findings:

> Teachers who reported that lack of basic skills was not a hindrance to their students' academic success, that lack of student discipline and parent support was not a problem, or that students could learn with the resources available also reported higher implementation than those who felt otherwise.

> Schools in which teachers reported strong principal leadership also reported much higher levels of implementation. We find that this variable was strongly correlated with teachers' reports of the level of resources—in terms of materials, funds, and time—available to them to implement designs.

> In general, levels of implementation were higher in those districts that were more supportive of the New American School designs and characterized by stability of district leadership.

Did we really need a research study to tell us that when students have better academic skills, good discipline, and parental support, program success is more likely than is the case without those attributes? Was special insight required to say that leadership, resources, and district support are all a good idea? In research parlance, these factors are confounding variables. Any assertion that one can draw a straight line from a program out of a box to student achievement without considering these factors is specious. In the context of this discussion, we must recognize that comprehensive school reform programs are not a strategy any more than a textbook, calculator, or desk is a strategy. When I hear a superintendent or board member claim that "our strategy is to get (insert your favorite brand name program here) into every building," then I know that strategic leadership is misunderstood or utterly absent.

Let us return to our definition of strategic leadership: the simultaneous acts of executing, evaluating, and reformulating strategies, and focusing organizational energy and resources on the most effective strategies. Comprehensive school reform models are potentially part of a strategy and, if well executed, part of your information system. But the leader must relate those decisions to mission and values quite apart from the claims made by a vendor. The leader must furthermore evaluate and reformulate strategy, including making modifications or completely eliminating any strategy that does not work. In the Memphis case, it was quite unlikely that simultaneously embracing every program constituted strategic leadership. It is certain that simultaneously eliminating every program constituted strategic leadership, unless the constellation of evidence was so perfectly aligned that the identical decision turned out to be appropriate in each and every case. Neither decision reflects consideration of information and focusing of energy and resources, which are at the heart of strategic leadership. In the next chapter, we explore the implications of strategic leadership for the school district as well as leaders at the state and national levels.

Leadership Reflections

1. What is your mission—not the mission of your organization, but your personal mission?

2. What is the mission of your organization? (Write it down exactly, even if you have to look it up in a long-neglected document.)

3. How does the answer to the first question fit with the answer to the second question?

4. Rewrite the answer to the second question so that it conforms to your personal mission and also meets the twin criteria of brevity and passion.

5. What is one example of a strategy you have personally led? Remember, a strategy is a description of decisions linked to your mission, information, and results.

6. What is one example of effective strategic leadership for which you have been responsible? Your description must clearly show evidence that you simultaneously executed, evaluated, and reformulated a strategy and that you focused organizational energy and resources on the most effective strategy.

Chapter Seven

Strategic Leadership in Action

Leadership Keys

The daily practice of strategic leadership

The federal perspective: standards, assessment, and accountability

The state perspective: freedom at a price

The district perspective: redefining educational accountability

Authors must regularly confront the truth of the maxim that it is easier to give advice than to take it. It is also easier to define terms than to operationalize them. In this chapter, I must accept both challenges, offering an operational definition of what strategic leadership means in practice and also presenting examples of where I have implemented strategic leadership.

Thucydides, the historian of the Peloponnesian Wars, warned us of the inherent bias in the historical accounts of those who win the battle. What I offer here is no victor's history; rather, I share, warts and all, examples of where the definition of strategic leadership has been used well and where it has foundered. I have always distrusted those autobiographical accounts that appear to claim, "If you can only be like me, then everything will be swell!" A more accurate guide for this chapter is, "If you will learn from my mistakes, as well as the mistakes and success I have observed in almost thirty years of leadership study, everything will not necessarily be swell, but you will approach each challenge with greater insight and more confidence."

There is a risk in this confessional approach. By revealing my own mistakes, some readers will conclude that this book is an exercise of the genre best described as "Do as I say, not as I do." An alternative conclusion is that we are all in the process of improving our leadership. Only through rigorous comparison of the difference between where we are to where we want to be can we improve our leadership abilities and the organizations for which we are responsible. Confession of error is the price of improvement, and this transparency is the example we owe to all of our colleagues.

Strategic Leadership in Action

Let us first return to our definitions. Strategy is a description of decisions linked to the mission, information, and results. Strategic leadership occurs in the course of the simultaneous acts of executing, evaluating, and reformulating strategies, and focusing organizational energy and resources on the most effective strategies. We begin with self-analysis of time and priorities; then we consider the extent to which those priorities lead to execution, evaluation, and reformulation of strategy. Finally, we consider the extent to which your leadership focuses organizational energy and resources on the most effective strategy.

Time, the Leader's Most Important Resource

When I ask leaders to consider their priorities, most of them are quick to come up with a list. Although the lists are, by and large, too long, at least the leaders are able to articulate priorities. We may speak about our mission and vision, our people, our families, and perhaps even our personal health all as important priorities in our lives. When we compare our calendars to how we spend our time, the difference between the illusion and the reality sets in. The best reflection of a leader's priorities is the calendar, particularly one that captures real-time allocation of the leader's most important resource, time. Try capturing for two weeks how you spend time, from the moment you wake up until the moment you fall asleep. The results may surprise you. In my case, I was able to consistently account for about sixteen hours a day. This seemed a little light, because it feels as if I get fewer than eight hours of sleep each night. Nevertheless, as I regularly encourage educational leaders to do, let the data speak (Figure 7.1).

The good news is that I appear to spend about a third of my time with my family. Lest anyone think that this qualifies me for a role in "Father Knows Best," I hasten to add that I included every trip to school and store as well as movies that we watched in silence. About a fifth of my waking hours were devoted to clients, the school systems around the world with which I have worked for the past several years. Fourteen percent of the time was devoted to research and writing, principally on the pages you are now reading, though I regularly wade through research on leadership, education, and organizational effectiveness even when it is not related to my own writing projects.

It is the rest of the graph that is disturbing. Fully 9 percent of my time is devoted to the category called "Travel NP," with the *NP*

Figure 7.1. Time Allocation Analysis

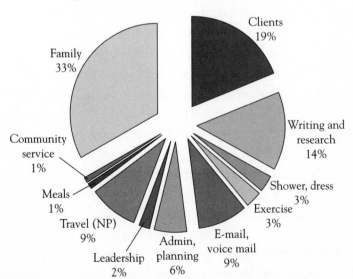

standing for nonproductive. I pride myself as someone who is ruth-less about time, always reading while standing in a line, making notes by hand when an airline does not allow computer use (or the computer batteries have run out), and even listening to unabridged books on tape when I'm in the subway. Nevertheless, there is a large number of hours that have been consumed in driving, flying, waiting in line, or otherwise traveling when I have not been able to categorize them for research, leadership, or any other more impor-tant category. Those hours are not completely idle, as I have waded through *The Story of Civilization, Greek Myths, From Dawn to Decadence*, and more than a few volumes of lighter fare as I travel and stand in line. Nevertheless, these hours represent a great deal of time in which I am not pursuing the most important tasks of the day.

Perhaps the worst inference from my analysis of time allocation—particularly for the author of a book on leadership—is that it appears that during the weeks of this time analysis I devoted only 2 percent of my time to activities categorized as leadership—the strategic planning, coaching, evaluating, and communicating that is at the heart of essential leadership tasks. In other words, I spent a bit less time on leadership than I spent running, shaving, or showering, and far less than I spent responding to e-mail and voice mail. I am not proud of this ratio, but I share it because I strongly suspect it is not much different from many readers. After a burst of energy on the development of strategies, in which the bulk of our time is devoted to meeting, thinking, and planning, we come to an implementation phase in which the percentage of our time devoted to coaching, encouraging, monitoring, and implementing those plans shrinks dramatically.

The display of data accompanied by confession of error is an empty exercise if we do not use the data to improve performance. In subsequent months, I have increased my allocation of leadership time to 12 percent, while decreasing nonproductive travel time to 3 percent. The balance remains imperfect, but the only way any of us can improve how we use time is to become acutely aware of how this precious resource is spent. Equipped with this knowledge, we can make regular refinements and improvements in our performance. When the leader sets a disciplined example, the rest of the organization will notice the value of time as well as the importance of time management disciplines.

If you would like to undertake your own time analysis, use the Leadership Time Log in Appendix B (form B.1). Within two weeks, you will have a clear idea of the extent to which your time reflects your priorities. An obsession with time is not necessary, but it is reasonable for you to treat your time with the same attention to detail that you would financial resources. People who read their bank statements and balance their checkbooks tend to have better ability to make a midcourse correction in their financial spending pattern than do people who never look at such data. Although you need not complete a time log every day, you should consider this two-week discipline at least once a year, and perhaps every quarter.

The Daily Disciplines of Strategic Leadership

Effective use of your time is a prerequisite for effective strategic leadership, but it is not sufficient to guarantee success. The daily disciplines of strategic leadership include five key steps that are ingrained in the daily practice of the strategic leader. These disciplines, summarized in Exhibit 7.1, are to (1) define objectives on the basis of

Exhibit 7.1. The Daily Disciplines of Leadership

1. *Define objectives on the basis of the mission.*
2. *Create standards of action.* What must the organization do?
3. *Develop an assessment tool.* How do you know if you are successful? How do you know if you are exemplary? How do know if you have not yet achieved success?
4. *Implement an accountability system.* Measure organizational results and the specific actions of individuals and of the organization that are intended to cause those results.
5. *Provide continuous feedback.* Analyze the relationship (or lack of relationship) between action and results, and refocus organizational energy and resources on the strategies that are most closely related to desired results.

the mission, (2) create standards of action, (3) develop an assessment tool, (4) implement an accountability system, and (5) provide continuous feedback. Let us explore each of these in detail.

Discipline One: Define Objectives on the Basis of the Mission. The mission of the organization must be brief and passionate, displaying the very reason for its existence. It encapsulates in a handful of words the reason people work there. It gives the leader the focal point around which people with widely differing points of view can be rallied. The objectives, however, must be established by the leader, who engages every element of the organization to focus on those objectives that support the mission. The mission of learning for all students, for example, entails specific objectives for teachers, bus drivers, curriculum designers, administrative assistants, special education directors, and food service workers.

There is an important distinction between a task list and clearly defined objectives based on a mission. Tasks are accomplished when they are checked off the traditional to-do list and the person making the assignment is satisfied. Objectives that are linked to the mission are different. As each objective is accomplished, the organization moves one step closer to achieving the mission. Individuals and organizations need clearly defined objectives, particularly if the leader has followed the advice of Collins and Porras (1994) to establish Big Hairy Audacious Goals, a less elegant echo of the words of Robert Browning:

> *Ah, but a man's reach should exceed his grasp,*
> *Or what's a heaven for?*
>
> —"Andrea del Sarto," line 97

There are some rules, absolute certainties, that surround consideration of leadership objectives. You can be certain, for example, that the potential supply of objectives that many people regard as a pretty good idea exceeds your available resources and time. You can further be certain that the total number of objectives in your organization right now exceeds the number of objectives that are explicitly linked to your mission. Thus the first step in strategic leadership is not necessarily a matter of generating more things to do, more objectives to be achieved. Rather, it involves rigorous review of your existing objectives and tasks to determine which are linked to the mission, which are not, and which ones require some modification. There is another reason that the daily disciplines of strategic leadership begin with objectives based on the mission. Leaders at every level in the organization are forced physically to look at the mission statement every single day. If it is not simple, brief, and compelling, then there will soon be a clarion call for modifying the mission into a statement worthy of this daily discipline and, more important, worthy of the engagement of the hearts and minds of everyone in the organization.

Discipline Two: Create Standards of Action. The word *standards* has been used so profligately that we must be careful in our definition. Is a standard just an expectation or a requirement? Is a standard something we hope for or demand? Is a standard subject to binary evaluation (we do it or we don't)? Or is it subtler, with varying degrees of accomplishment along a continuum from none at all to a level of performance far exceeding the standard? Because of the confusion such questions raise and owing to the need for strategic leadership to be clear, transparent, and easy to understand, the discipline for "standards of action" is unambiguous in its answers to each question.

A standard of action is a requirement. In the school cafeteria, a standard of action is that employees wash their hands prior to touching food; in the board room, a standard of action is that items must be on the agenda to be discussed; in the classroom, a standard of action is that students and teachers must observe safety rules. Although we get to the subtleties of assessing leadership action in the next step, creating standards of action sets up a binary evaluation system allowing the leader to answer yes or no to the question of whether the action standard is achieved. Did I begin the day with a prioritized task list? Did I devote the majority of my time to completing an objective that was related to our mission? Did I identify and eliminate a task, program, or operation that was not supporting our mission? The responses do not allow equivocation, and every organization needs the discipline of such standards of action. They are the organizational safety net. If the leader asks his colleagues whether a standard or action has been achieved, he should expect a clear and definitive answer.

Discipline Three: Develop an Assessment Tool. For each objective, the leader must know in advance what success looks like. An organizational vision statement is a long-term indication of what success means, but it can only be viewed from a distance, as the mast of a ship on the horizon. An assessment tool, by contrast, creates a vision of success for a specific organizational activity. Consider the example of a school system that wants to improve classroom assessment, the heart of improving teacher expectations of students. The initiative might begin with a vaguely worded goal such as "improve classroom assessment," but now the leader must define what such improvement means in a way that is absolutely clear to every classroom professional and school administrator. A standard of action—totally objective and not subject to analysis—might be that "each ninth grade algebra class will use a common end-of-semester assessment for students, and the results of those assessments will be reported within five days after the end of each semester." But if we are to really improve classroom assessment, progress will be made along a continuum from relatively poor classroom practice, through teaching behavior that was originally expected by the leader, to performance that is distinguished. To create this vision of success along a continuum of performance, the leader will describe the levels of assessment success, such as those listed in Exhibit 7.2.

Leaders can create the same assessment for themselves. For example, if the challenge is time management, the leader might

Exhibit 7.2. Discipline Three: Develop an Assessment Tool

Goal: improving classroom assessment practice

Distinguished practice

A review of teacher-created assessments reveals use of multiple measurements (at least three) of each essential concept and different assessment methods, including multiple-choice, extended written response, demonstration, and oral presentations. This teacher collaboratively evaluates student work with colleagues at least weekly. The teacher regularly helps colleagues improve assessment practice and shares new assessment items. High expectations linked to state standards are evident in all assessments and evaluation practice.

Proficient practice

A review of teacher assessment practice reveals creation of at least eight teacher-made assessments and regular use of multiple-choice and extended response assessment items. The assessments are clearly linked to state standards. This teacher participates in collaborative scoring of student work at least monthly.

Approaching proficiency

A review of teacher assessment practice reveals almost exclusive reliance on assessments created by external sources, such as textbooks or other teachers. Although multiple methods are used, there is unbalanced reliance on multiple-choice assessment. Collaborative scoring occurred fewer than nine times during the year.

Not meeting standard

A review of teacher assessment practice reveals no teacher-created assessments, or those that have been created are not related to state academic standards. There is little or no evidence of multiple method assessment. This teacher does not participate in collaborative scoring of student work, or participation was limited to attendance without active interaction with colleagues.

---

develop an assessment describing in detail the behaviors and activities associated with exemplary time management, those associated with proficient time management, and a vivid description of what it looks like when a leader fails to manage time well. Many important elements of leadership behavior and practice can be analyzed on such a continuum; this is far more helpful for self-reflection and in coaching others than a simple checklist of characteristics.

In any endeavor, your colleagues must know, "What does success look like?" Anyone on a family road trip knows that the human inclination to ask "Are we there yet?" begins very early in life. With an assessment for each project or task, the leader can give a much better answer than we gave to the incessantly inquiring child (who, after all, was never satisfied with "In a little while"). We can and must do better, giving specific answers for a vision of success and also with absolute clarity a vision of what is not acceptable.

Discipline Four: Implement an Accountability System. The strategic leader regards accountability differently than does the typical leader. Even apparently effective leaders who regard themselves as "results-driven" or "data-driven" are not able to make strategic decisions if the results and data on which they focus are typically a set of test scores. The strategic leader focuses on causes as well as effects and thus uses accountability not as an annual report card but as a daily guide to improved student achievement and leadership decision making. The leader does not want an accountability report in the car to announce, somewhere in the middle of the New Mexico desert, "You are out of gas." She wants a series of accountability reports to guide her, give her multiple early warning signs, many opportunities to change direction or get more resources. Most accountability reports are an educational autopsy; the strategic leader uses accountability reports as a physical— a guide to improved organizational and individual health (Reeves, 2002b).

We explore the components of an effective accountability system later in this chapter, but in the context of the daily disciplines of the strategic leader accountability simply means identifying and focusing on just a few variables that are clearly linked to the most important strategies of the organization. By having daily access to these key accountability indicators, the leader is also able to ensure that many other people in the system are watching the same numbers. Think of it as a dashboard; you can't drive the car well if the only gauge available tells the fuel level, since you are unaware of the car overheating, or running out of oil, or going too fast. If the car has a hundred gauges, you are unable to find the speedometer and fuel gauge when you need to. Thus the leader's employment of an accountability system as a daily discipline refers to selecting the few indicators that are most important. Here are some examples that an educational leader at the system level might want to have daily, particularly for a district whose mission statement emphasizes educational achievement and equity:

- Student attendance
- Faculty and administrator attendance
- Noncertified staff attendance
- Number of days without a violent incident or safety violation
- Percentage of students with zero disciplinary infractions
- Percentage of students proficient or higher in reading, as measured by an assessment administered less than twelve months ago
- Percentage of nonproficient students who are receiving specifically targeted additional assistance beyond that provided in the regular curriculum

By tracking daily, weekly, and monthly trends in these indicators (so few that the leader can carry them around on a three-by-five card), the leader sees the relationship between these daily "antecedents of excellence" and the larger system-level concerns of achievement and safety. Let me emphasize: they are not obvious. The majority of leaders I speak with every day—and I have spoken to thousands—do not know the answers to these questions unless someone goes to extra effort and renders a formal report. If accountability becomes a daily discipline, then the day doesn't start without these numbers, and changes in them that are significant are likely to influence how the leader spends time, allocates resources, and makes decisions. It is perhaps obvious that a banker or businessperson regards cash as something important to watch, but the best bankers and businesspeople I know can tell you daily how much cash they have. It is their equivalent of student and staff attendance—obviously important, but infrequently monitored by too many leaders.

The final benefit of the daily discipline of accountability is that the strategic leader models fidelity to the standards to which everyone in the organization must adhere. As a fundamental moral principle, we should not expect third graders to be more accountable than the adults in the system; nor should teachers and administrators be more accountable than the superintendent and board. When the leader demonstrates daily commitment to measurable accountability—not merely an annual recitation of scores and data but a daily commitment to understanding both causes and effects of student achievement—then it is apparent to everyone else in the organization that the leader establishes a model for constructive accountability.

Discipline Five: Provide Continuous Feedback. Inextricably linked to constructive use of accountability is provision of feedback that is timely, accurate, and meaningful. By linking accountability measurements to feedback, the strategic leader can demonstrate the link between strategies, information, and decisions. However obvious this may seem, the practice of linking feedback to decision making is uncommon and certainly not obvious. Even with the national trend toward "data-driven decision-making" seminars, we have only created a large number of leaders who have more data and may be better informed about the problems that they face, but they are rarely making different decisions. Consider this dialogue I had recently with a leader:

Reeves: So your data analysis revealed 128 sixth grade students who are two or more grade levels below where they should be. How will that affect their curriculum for next year?
Leader: Well, we're going to share that data with the teachers and principals.

Reeves: Yes, but how will that affect the curriculum of the students? How will their time be spent differently? How will their learning be structured differently on the basis of this clear need?

Leader: Well, we're going to have another data-driven decision-making seminar and share that information with the teachers.

Reeves: Yes—but the teachers probably already know that these 128 students are poor readers—they see them every day. Teachers don't make schedule and curriculum changes. How will things change for the students? We have a crisis in the making for seventh and eighth grade. How will your information be used to avoid that crisis?

Leader: Well, we're just not quite there yet.

Conversations such as this reflect a belligerent indifference to facts. This is not data-driven decision making. It is not even data-free decision making, though that prevails in many schools. It is perhaps best labeled as "data-disregarded decision making." It is as if the same leader steps onto the scale in the doctor's office, listens to a solemn lecture on the dangers of obesity and diabetes, and, having nodded gravely in apparent agreement with the lecturing physicians, reaches into a briefcase for a pack of Twinkies, a can of beer, and a Marlboro.

Feedback is not about transmission of information. It is about using that information to change us. Terry Thompson did his midyear evaluations of administrators by asking a single compelling question: What are you going to do differently in the spring semester than you did in the fall semester? This is a data-rich district, and principals' offices were adorned with charts and graphs. The question remains, what will they do with the data? If you want to have a room full of leaders grow quiet very quickly, ask them to be prepared to announce in the next five minutes the answer to these three questions:

1. What will you do differently from what you did last year?
2. What will you stop doing that you did last year?
3. How and when will you know that you are making progress?

If the answer to the first question is a list of initiatives and the second question remains unanswered, then the new initiatives are doomed. If the answer to the third question does not include measurable results produced at frequent intervals—the daily disciplines of accountability and feedback—then we should not expect anything to change.

These daily disciplines—objectives, standards, assessment, accountability, and feedback—have become burdened with jargon-laden process and unnecessary complexity. Cars are complex, but we can drive one and monitor a clearly limited set of indicators. A school system may be more complex than a car (though we forget that the computing power in a car of current vintage probably exceeds the technology of an entire school district of a decade ago), but a school system is not more complex than a Boeing 777 or an aircraft carrier or a Fortune 500 corporation or a major nonprofit institution. All of these complex systems have in common the need for a strategic leader to focus on those decisions, objectives, and measurements that move the system to accomplishment of its mission. This does not happen only with annual planning meetings, but with daily discipline. In the next section, we meet some women and men who are examples of strategic leadership.

Alignment of Priorities with Actions

Just as analysis of time can betray the difference between actions and priorities, so also analysis of effective leadership action can display the link between leadership priorities and specific activity demonstrating the leader's application of effective strategic leadership. In the examples given here, some of the nation's most effective educational leaders—in systems large and small, including districts, counties, and states—demonstrate that strategic leadership is not a theory but daily integration of priorities with action. In each example, leadership actions that might otherwise have seemed isolated can be viewed as part of a broader context. Whether the action is the mundane evaluation of a principal, a visit to a classroom, evaluation of a curriculum, or purposeful sharing of effective teaching practice, each leader is an example of the link between strategy and action.

Terry Thompson, superintendent of Wayne Township Metropolitan School Corporation in Indianapolis, recently shared his evaluations of principals and senior administrators. Two remarkable characteristics jumped out at me from a review of these documents. First, the focus of each evaluation was clearly on student achievement, with a discussion of specific leadership practices that were related to student achievement. Second, these were among the few leadership evaluations I had ever seen that make specific reference to research and professional development linked to student achievement. This was far beyond a gentle warning that "test scores had better improve or you are in trouble." Rather, the evaluations were specific coaching guides that included a blueprint for continued improvement.

Bill Habermehl, superintendent of the Orange County (California) Office of Education, has responsibility for almost half a million students, but he pays detailed attention to curriculum choices for them. If they are permitted to choose the path of least resistance, it might indicate that the adults in the system are validating inappropriately low expectations. As the first in his family to go to college, Habermehl knows about the power of high expectations and the peril of allowing an adolescent to make an unwise choice. When he tried to drop algebra in high school, his mother protested to school officials. Though she might not have known what algebra was, she knew it was important for her son's future success and she insisted that he not be permitted to avoid it.

Today, as a successful leader of a complex educational system, Habermehl remains relentlessly focused on effective action. He prefers an informal walk-around encounter to a formal staff meeting and time in the classroom with real students to the artificiality of a briefing by administrators. "If I were to write a book for leaders," Habermehl concluded, "It would have 399 blank pages and on the

400th page would be the words, 'Just do it.'" He exemplifies one of the principles of excellence articulated by Peters and Waterman (1982) that has stood the test of time: a "bias for action."

Chris Wright, now superintendent in Hazelton, Missouri, and formerly the leader of the Riverview Gardens School District outside of St. Louis, won national recognition simultaneously for improved student achievement and improved labor-management relations. She dramatically simplified the planning process, provided consistent feedback to everyone in the system, and presented visible evidence of monthly improvement in targeted goals for each school and for the system as a whole.

Ray Simon, director of the Arkansas Department of Education, pioneered a new balance between state leadership in student achievement and local selection of strategies to achieve common goals. Under his leadership, schools with a very high percentage of students eligible for free and reduced lunch in both rural and urban areas made dramatic improvement on state and national indicators of achievement. Moreover, he was the architect of educational policies that gained broad bipartisan support in a political environment that had been notably fractious. One of the most interesting initiatives that Simon led was at the heart of effective strategic leadership: continuous evaluation and reconsideration of previous programs. Statewide initiatives were not merely launched with great fanfare and forgotten but were subjected to rigorous evaluation for the degree of implementation and the level of results achieved. From those evaluations, midcourse corrections could be made and a series of "lessons learned" were established for the benefit of present and future leaders.

Heidi Laabs, director of instruction in Waukesha, Wisconsin, is into her fifth year of improving student achievement through a focus on standards-based performance assessment. Many districts claim to have such a focus, but Laabs is unusual in that each year she publishes samples of the best work of teachers and students and posts them on the Internet. In this way, she honors and publicizes the work of her classroom professionals, while sharing with the district and the world the fruits of that extraordinary effort. More-over, as time goes on, the district and outside observers can observe continuous progress toward the narrowly focused goal of improved student achievement through improved classroom assessments based on state academic standards.

Stan Scheer, now in his third superintendent's position, is one of the most relentlessly focused leaders I have ever seen. Irrespec-tive of the changes that confront him in politics, finances, stan-dards, and testing, he maintains a focus on a very few areas, such as achievement and financial stability, which dominate every plan-ning session, board meeting, and strategic action documentation. He continues a practice he began as a rookie administrator: putting himself on the substitute teacher roster so that he regularly sees the world from the viewpoint of the students and teachers.

Deanna Housfeld, now retired from the Milwaukee public schools, was the author of the brilliantly titled "One Plan," in which every central office request was reduced to a single docu-ment. In a district with almost two hundred buildings and more than one hundred thousand students, she saved literally thousands of person-hours by avoiding repeated requests for the same infor-mation. In addition, she forced systematic examination of the ques-tions, "Why do we need that information, anyway?" and "If we really do need that information, can't we just get it once a year and then not bug the principals anymore?"

Anita Poston, recently retired president of the board of educa-tion for the Norfolk (Virginia) public schools, is one of the few educational leaders in the nation who have successfully narrowed the focus of their planning to a single objective: improved student achievement for all students, with "all" meaning "all." Just as important, she has led the way in establishing standards for board members and the board of education as a whole, so that every action of the district, from policy making to system-level leader-ship to classroom teaching, is aligned toward achievement of a single goal. Under the leadership of superintendent John Simpson and Chief Academic Officer Thomas Lockamy, the district represents one of the nation's most dramatic success stories, with almost three dozen schools making great improvements in student achievement. This is all the more remarkable because it has occurred in an environment of economic deprivation, a history of racial division, and the social upheaval associated with the large number of military personnel in Norfolk being deployed after September 11, 2001.

In Columbus, Ohio, the district was faced with chronically low student achievement and the need for better feedback before annual state tests. They developed a districtwide writing assessment because it would serve as a predictor for state writing assessment and also be an opportunity for teachers to simulate the same assessment conditions, allowing students to learn from this experience and thus prepare for the higher-stakes state-level assessment. Columbus leaders and teachers received timely feedback from the district writing scoring team about their successes and the needs of their students; thus they could make immediate intervention decisions and implement specific actions during the months before the state writing assessment. Interestingly, this linkage of specific classroom-level decisions to system-level strategies bore fruit not only in the quality of student writing but also in the frequency and quality of teacher collaboration. In addition, improvements in student written expression ability helped them achieve gains in other areas of the state proficiency tests: social studies, reading, and mathematics.

Daily Disciplines in Practice

The worksheet in Appendix C is a convenient way for you to practice the daily disciplines of strategic leadership. You will find some days where your objectives are lost, where you can't find important information, and even if you find great information you fail to use it for effective feedback. Nevertheless, only by persisting in the daily disciplines can you make progress toward your journey of becoming the most effective strategic leader you can be.

Leadership Journal

These cases of effective alignment of leadership priorities with the daily activities of the leader are extraordinary because they are rare. Moreover, each of these leaders readily confesses that there are many days on which the alignment between priorities and leadership action is far from perfect. It is, however, precisely this understanding that allows these leaders to be effective. They are willing to engage in reflection and thereby improve their level of understanding. They can only make midcourse corrections—simultaneous execution and evaluation of strategies, the hallmark of strategic leadership—if they are willing to take time to engage in reflection. One of the best ways to encourage structured reflection is a leadership journal, particularly if you are willing to discuss your reflections with a trusted colleague, leadership coach, mentor, or other person who asks the hard questions and listens seriously to your ideas, doubts, fears, and hopes. Journal entries need not be epic in length or possess Freudian insight. Rather, they should contain your brief and absolutely honest responses to some essential questions. You will want to develop your own questions that keep you focused on the issues most important to you, but the Leadership Journal in Appendix B (form B.2) is one model. Here are the questions on that form:

1. What did you learn today?
2. Who did you nurture today?
3. What difficult issue did you confront today?
4. What is your most important challenge right now?
5. What did you do today to make progress on your most important challenge?

The New Federal Impact on Education

In the early days of 2002, more than 90 percent of the members of the U.S. Congress passed the most sweeping reform of federal education legislation in the past thirty years. Both candidates for president in the 2000 election favored use of academic content standards, testing in reading and math, and significantly improved educational accountability systems (Reeves, 2001a). Therefore it was little surprise that both parties reached substantial agreement on all portions of the education legislation. Once the contentious issue of school vouchers was removed from the proposals, the parties came to agreement and the bill signing was simultaneously hailed by President George W. Bush and Senator Edward Kennedy, two people who otherwise do not share many enthusiasms.

For the most part, federal legislation gives broad latitude to the states for spending federal dollars, provided that the states meet certain criteria. They include the requirement that federal education investment be devoted exclusively to programs that are supported by scientifically based research (Reeves, 2002a). In addition, each state must establish rigorous academic content standards and establish a mechanism for students to be tested in at least the areas of reading and mathematics in a manner that reflects those state-level academic standards.

Federal legislation carries a broad impact in the areas of standards and testing and also in special education, where federal mandates have for a quarter-century far outstripped federal funding.

For the most part, the federal legislation and the accompanying implementing regulations at the state and federal levels were only a piece of the data for strategic leadership. The other elements of strategic leadership, including the linking of decisions to priorities and information, are left to the individual school system. Despite its commitment to scientific research, the federal legislation does not attend to gathering any "cause" variables systematically or nationally. Rather, each state must gather test scores—effect variables that reflect a variety of causes in the form of leadership, teaching, and curriculum strategic. Because the federal legislation does require gathering information on the socioeconomic status and ethnic identity of students, too many observers may conclude that those factors are the cause of student achievement. Later in this chapter we explore use of constructive accountability systems that allow the strategic leader to emerge from unenlightening rumination over test scores and engage in the far more useful practice of holistic accountability (Reeves, 2002b).

Federalism in Practice: Freedom at a Price

One significant impact at the federal level is the remarkable reduction in the sheer number of federal programs. In dozens of cases, discretion that had been previously reserved exclusively to the federal education department was, in the new legislation, ceded to the states. Enthusiasts label this the "new federalism" and laud exclusion of the federal bureaucracy from educational decision making at the local level. Skeptics note that, at least in some states, the law has simply substituted one inefficient and unwieldy bureaucracy (at the federal level) for another inefficient and unwieldy bureaucracy (at the state level). Other critics claim that the state departments of education are remarkably uneven in their level of technical expertise, staffing, and size. Thus some may be ill-equipped for the complexity and challenge imposed on them by the new federal legislation. "Local control" is a common staple of political speeches from the local school board to the presidential campaign, but the actual practice of administering multibillion-dollar programs in a complex tapestry of federal, state, and local regulations requires administration (none dare call it bureaucracy), and the functionality of state and local educational administration is inconsistent.

Redefining Educational Accountability in School Districts

Although some observers argue that the state and federal testing programs of the past several years have largely taken away the accountability prerogatives that previously resided with local school districts (Paul Houston, personal interview, Mar. 28, 2002), another point of view holds that the growing emphasis on test scores at the state and federal levels makes it all the more imperative that local school districts develop comprehensive accountability systems that place educational data, including test scores, into the appropriate context.

The opportunity for the strategic leader to implement educational accountability has never been greater; nor has it ever been more important. State policy makers overwhelmingly depend on test scores to evaluate educational effectiveness (Gullatt and Ritter, 2002). Although some states also use site visits and demographic data as part of their evaluation, systematic measurement of teaching, leadership, and curriculum practices is rare. There are, however, some shining examples of educational accountability systems that are constructive and comprehensive (Reeves, 2000a; 2002b). Although use of state tests is clearly a part of educational accountability, they need not constitute the entire system. Strategic leaders have the opportunity—and the obligation—to place tests scores in context. Indeed, they cannot use information to make strategic decisions if they only have test score data. They must also have information on the processes and practices that lead to those scores.

Any state-of-the-art educational accountability system includes three levels of information. The first is the required information on student achievement, attendance, safety, and other indicators that relate to the entire educational system. These are the "effect" variables. The second level of the accountability system includes indicators that vary with each school. These "cause" variables reflect specific teaching, leadership, and curriculum practices that meet the individual needs of each school. For example, the entire district may have as an indicator the scores on fourth grade reading tests. But the leaders and faculty at Jefferson Elementary School have noticed that they have a particular challenge in summarization of nonfiction text. Therefore they create a school-based assessment to address this particular challenge. By recording the percentage of students proficient or higher on this assessment each month, teachers at Jefferson can identify students who need assistance and conduct effective and timely intervention before the test. Moreover, by reporting their results of the school-based assessment in the comprehensive accountability system, the district leadership can determine the extent to which school-based strategies are linked to improvement in student achievement and other systemwide goals.

The third tier of a comprehensive educational accountability system is a narrative description for each school. This qualitative description helps the reader understand the relationship between the tier one effect variables and the tier two cause variables. In addition, the school narrative is the qualitative lens through which quantitative data can be better understood. Many aspects of organizational climate (student-teacher relationships, parental involvement, social environment) are best described in words rather than numbers. The school narrative is an opportunity for a balance of qualitative and quantitative information, and it is upon this balance that careful and complete analysis by strategic leaders depends.

For a more detailed examination of creating a comprehensive and constructive accountability system, two resources may be useful. *Holistic Accountability: Serving Students, Schools, and Community* (Reeves, 2002b) is a brief overview of comprehensive accountability designed for policy makers and senior leaders. *Accountability in Action: A Blueprint for Learning Organizations* (Reeves, 2000a) is a full examination of the accountability process and is appropriate for administrators and teachers who are personally responsible for creating a new accountability system. Finally, the *Video Journal of Education,* vol. 1001, *Accountability for Student Learning* (Reeves, 2000b), includes spontaneous and unrehearsed film of board members, school leaders, parents, and students creating comprehensive accountability systems and enjoying the benefits of such a system.

Effective accountability systems recognize what Hammer (2001) calls the "principle of obliquity," in which the link between causes and effects is not immediately obvious. An accountability system that focuses exclusively on results but does not let each participant in the system know his specific role in influencing results is an exercise in futility. The path between causes and results is not obvious but, as Hammer suggests, oblique. In the context of education, for example, a cause variable could be student involvement in extracurricular activities, which in turn leads to improved attendance, which is associated with improved student-teacher communication, which is associated with greater likelihood that the student requests help and that the teacher quickly notices and reacts to student difficulty, which is associated with improved academic achievement.

Without such an analysis, it is not obvious that the football coach, drama club advisor, and art teacher all have the opportunity to play an important role in improving academic achievement. Anne Bryant (personal interview, Apr. 3, 2002) argues persuasively that accountability is more than test scores; factors such as emotional intelligence for students and adults in the system are vitally important. These are not fluff or "soft" or beyond measurement, but vitally important indicators for systemwide success. An accountability system must recognize the importance of the nonobvious indicators and the oblique paths that occur between causes and effects.

Leadership Reflections

1. Identify an example you have personally observed of strategic leadership—a leadership action or series of decisions that linked decision making with information, results, and the mission. Moreover, this example demonstrated simultaneous execution and evaluation of the decisions so that resources and time could be allocated in the most effective manner possible. Explain your example to a colleague without calling it "strategic leadership," and ask your colleague to notice what the decision maker did that was unusual or particularly effective.

2. Consider your own responsibilities right now. Describe your own daily disciplines of strategic leadership. (If you prefer, use the worksheet in Appendix C rather than this writing space.)

Objectives on the basis of the mission:

Standards of action:

Assessment:

Accountability:

Feedback:

Part Three

Leadership in Action

Chapter Eight

The Daily Disciplines of Leadership

Leadership Keys

Decide what is within your control

Gain control of time

Leadership hygiene: the Daily Prioritized Task List

Linking leadership time to student achievement

Leadership time is inextricably linked to student achievement. Every element of achievement, from professional development to organization to assessment to collaboration, requires an enormous investment of time. If an educational leader fails to use time wisely, in a manner that is relentlessly focused on improved student achievement and implementation of academic standards, then a thousand other tasks intrude. Time management on the part of the leader is the difference between the theory of standards and the practice of standards-based leadership.

The effective leader uses time differently than an ineffective leader does. This single sentence sums up my observation of thousands of leaders in a range of educational settings. My observations are consistent with those of many who have studied leaders in organizations far afield of education, from Peter Drucker to Tom Peters and Margaret Wheatley. The most effective leaders do not necessarily have more money, fewer unions, more enlightened stakeholders, or longer days. Rather, they know those areas where their decisions have the maximum impact on essential results, and they focus their time on those areas within their control. Just as the standards-based leader articulates standards for student achievement and faculty instructional strategies, she must also create and maintain standards for her own mastery of the critical leadership resource of time.

I frequently hear leaders complain how little they can control: "I'm supposed to be the leader, but the union controls working conditions, the central office controls the budget and maintenance, and parents and students control three-fourths of every day. What can I really control?" The concern is a fair one, but it does not explain how two schools in the same district with the same union, same central office, same demographic characteristics, and same constraints from parents and students can have dramatically differing results. Under the same union contract, teachers have different schedules, students have varying levels of intervention, and the focus of faculty meetings and professional development are dramatically divergent. The only explanation for this is that the leaders take the same conditions and constraints and are able to implement strategic decisions that yield extraordinary results. More than anything else, exceptional leaders use time differently.

Essentials of Leadership Time Management

A review of many time management systems reveals a few key common ingredients. These systems vary widely in their format and include sophisticated computer programs (GoldMine, Act!, Microsoft Outlook), home-made time management lists using a computer spreadsheet program, formal planning systems (planners and organizers by Franklin/Covey, DayTimer, Day Runner), plain legal pads, and three-by-five index cards. Despite these differences, however, there are remarkably similarities in the processes of effective time management. Over the course of a few decades of studying effective time management, I am increasingly convinced that this is an organizational discipline that is absolutely essential. If the leader does not organize time wisely, priorities are ignored, goals are rendered impotent, strategy is irrelevant, and grandiloquent oratory about educational imperatives is inevitably hypocritical. No leader can expect teachers and students to organize time and set priorities unless the leader sets an example. Whatever the computer program or stationery, here are the keys to effective leadership time management.

Master Task List (Appendix B.3)

Write all tasks on a single list and all scheduled obligations on a single calendar. The leader cannot have one list and calendar for school, another for central office requirements, one for community service activities, and yet another one for family activities. A cardinal principle of effective time management is a single calendar for all activities and a single list for all tasks. I have seen busy public officials, attorneys, school superintendents, and business leaders adhere to this rule. They could never manage the multiple demands of family, community, and professional obligations if they did not keep a single calendar.

One great advantage of a computerized program is that the space needed for a single day automatically expands to meet the requirements of that day. But even with a manual system, the low-tech solution to the imperative for a single combined calendar is (not surprisingly) a calendar with larger space for each day. Every task goes on this list, including phone calls to be returned, phone calls to be initiated, letters to be returned, and e-mails that did not receive an immediate response. If a large chunk of time requirement, such as that associated with e-mail and voice mail, is tracked on another list, then the entire principle of prioritized time management breaks down. Everything goes on one list. That's the rule.

Break Projects into Tasks

Anything on the task list that cannot be accomplished in a single block of time is not a task, but a project. Each leader identifies what an appropriate block of time is, but it would hardly ever be more than three hours. Thus if something on your list requires more than three hours it is not a task, but a project. Projects should listed on separate project tracking sheet (form B.5 in Appendix B).

Prioritize and Date Each Task

A simple system of A, B, C suffices. Tasks with an A priority are important and must be accomplished. They may not require immediate action, but they are not discretionary. As examples, a statement for an expulsion hearing, or completing an evaluation form for a colleague, or a comment on a budget may be a task a week or more into the future, but each is absolutely essential and thus deserves A priority.

A good rule of thumb is that any leader cannot have more than six A-level tasks on a single day. If your task list contains dozens of A's (as mine occasionally does), then there are only two choices: change some of the A's to a B priority, or defer completion of the A-level tasks to a date on which there are six or fewer A tasks. Tasks with a B priority usually require leadership participation, but if there is limited time, they give way to A tasks.

Tasks with a C priority represent requests for leadership action, but they are not necessarily tasks that can be accomplished only by the leader. These include responding to many incoming e-mail, voice-mail, and regular mail messages, as well as requests that may or may not rise to the level of leadership importance. By writing C-level tasks on the master list, the leader is cognizant of the demands on time but also faces the inevitable fact that there are more demands than time available. At least once a day, C-level tasks are either delayed, assigned to someone else, or discarded. Because an effective task list always includes the date the task was added to the calendar, the leader can quickly and easily identify the tasks that are obsolete or no longer require action.

Sort Tasks in Priority and Date Order

Some time management systems require that the leader perform this function manually every day, and I know of leaders of very large organizations who find this manual process useful. The physical act of writing the most important tasks the first thing every morning or the last thing every evening places a framework around the entire day. Moreover, the demand for physical writing of tasks forces some abandonment of obsolete tasks, simply because rewriting tasks every day is too tedious. Paradoxically, it is this requirement for tedious reentry of tasks on the master list that actually saves time through effective focus and prioritization. Automated systems can grow by leaps and bounds, eventually including hundreds of tasks, because new tasks are added but old ones are rarely eliminated. If you use an automated system, the discipline of daily task review, prioritization, and culling of obsolete tasks is absolutely essential. The two-way sorting that I recommend—sorting by priority and by date—allows the leader to confront those tasks that are several weeks old.

Highlight Today's List

From the many tasks on today's list (and possibly from the many A-level tasks on the list), identify the six most important for today. I know of leaders who do this deliberately on a three-by-five index card that they carry around throughout the day. Before they accept interruptions or commit to completing a new task, they must confront whether the new addition is more important than their top six priorities for that day. Leaders who start each day claiming to have twenty or more "top priorities" are perpetually frustrated and anxious—surely victims of stress. Because they persist in the illusion that they can accomplish more than is humanly possible, they delay reassigning tasks, delegating to colleagues, or communicating with others that the tasks will not be accomplished on time. Thus their frustration and stress becomes a communicable disease, spreading from the leader to subordinates and colleagues throughout the organization. A sample Daily Prioritized Task List is form B.4 in Appendix B.

Work Today's List in Priority Order

No matter how obvious this may sound, most leaders fail to follow it. They start the day with a prioritized task list, are handed a stack of phone messages and the morning mail, and then listen to a dozen voice mail messages. By the time the well-intentioned leader has returned calls, answered mail, and taken incoming calls, hours have passed and not a single second has been devoted to the putative top priority of the day.

Commitment to working today's list in priority order implies clear recognition that not every voice mail, telephone message, e-mail, and letter is of equal importance. An e-mail system that beeps with every incoming note, whether it is a junk-mail solicitation or a critical note from a colleague, invites distortion of prioritization. There is no substitute for the rule of working the prioritized list in priority order.

Conduct a Prioritized Task Audit at Least Once a Week

Leaders are responsible not only for their own time management decisions, but also for those of colleagues. At least once a week, and preferably more often, a brief stand-up meeting should be held by top leaders in any organization in which the top six tasks are shared.

The key question that leaders must ask of one another is this: "Do your top priorities as reflected on the task list really reflect the top priorities of our organization?" If the leader works himself to the point of exhaustion and does not devote most of his energy to the highest priorities, then he should expect no merit badge for time management. Effectiveness, not exhaustion, is the hallmark of great time management.

Guidelines for Maintaining Your System Leadership Focus

First, find one time management system, and then stick with it.

The leader who flits from one system to another may display neat forms and have poor time management skills. Although the vendors of time management programs and forms do not like to hear it, consistent application of a system using the guidelines presented in this chapter is more important than the software or the forms. Mark McCormick operates one of the largest consulting organizations in the world using two legal pads, updated every day, for his prioritized daily task lists. As Hyrum Smith built the Franklin Institute into the world's leading time management program, eventually merging with Stephen Covey's organization to form Franklin/Covey, he used hand entries to create a daily prioritized task list in his Franklin Planner. Other leaders use a Palm Pilot or index cards, or a personal diary. The keys to effectiveness are the same: all tasks are centralized in a single location, prioritized, and worked in priority order.

Second, answer e-mail only twice a day.

If you have a computer that beeps with illusory urgency with every incoming e-mail, turn the alarm off, or if necessary turn the sound and speakers off. No one who sends e-mail has a right to expect an answer in minutes (although some senders of e-mail maintain such an absurd presumption). Think of it this way: if you were in a meeting with the school board, observing a classroom, or tutoring a child, then you would not interrupt those sessions each time a piece of junk mail arrived. The work you are doing on your top six priorities is of equal importance; it cannot be interrupted by e-mail. If your e-mail has an automated sorter, then it is possible to sort incoming mail in priority order on the basis of the sender or subject.

One good prioritization decision is to move anything that is a copy or "cc" to you to the bottom of the priority list. I know some senior leaders who simply reject all copied e-mail, operating on the theory that the sender has an obligation to communicate directly with whomever the intended recipient is, and that no "cc" line ought to be required to convey a sense of urgency. I receive close to one hundred e-mails every day, yet two sessions of thirty to forty-five minutes each are sufficient to stay on top of this burden.

Third, answer voice mail only three times a day, entering calls on the task list in priority order.

Voice mail can be retrieved and prioritized at selected times, with a typical schedule including morning, before lunch, and late afternoon. Because not all incoming calls are of equal priority, they can be addressed in priority order to forward to other colleagues for an appropriate response.

Fourth, answer only urgent and important mail daily; save all other mail for a weekly review.

Some mail deserves the attention of a same-day response, but a large amount of it is truly junk. My mail goes into three drawers: A for letters requiring an immediate response, B for professional literature I wish to read, and C for everything else. I only look at the C drawer once a week and typically fill two trash cans within ten minutes as I dump the vast majority of the C drawers without even opening the envelopes. There are some bulk mail items of interest—perhaps one in one hundred—and those can be quickly opened, considered, and added to the prioritized list or discarded. Everything else is trash and does not deserve the time required to open and read them.

Fifth, schedule a two-hour block of "project work time" at least once a week.

Once you settle into this habit, you will want to do it more frequently. Leaders who regularly engage in this practice report that they get more done in two focused and uninterrupted hours than in a full day in which they attempt to carry out a project but face constant interruptions. In most cases, the commitment to avoiding interruption can only be kept if the leader retreats to a physically separate space, such as a faculty work area, library, or conference room.

The voice mail and e-mail can accumulate for a couple of hours, just as it does if the leader is in a meeting or working with students.

What I Use

Because time is such a vexing challenge for many leaders, they frequently ask me what I use. My system is hardly perfect, but I am happy to share it as it is inexpensive and available to anyone whose computer includes a spreadsheet program. I have experimented with many systems. For many years now, I have used a system that allows me to balance the demands of a busy family, more than eighty speaking engagements each year, an average of two books and six articles written each year, voluminous correspondence with educators and school leaders throughout the world, and the complex organizational demands of the Center for Performance Assessment. It is a spreadsheet with three columns: the priority (A, B, or C), the task description, and the date the engagement started. The worksheet for my tasks is named "Reeves" and the same file contains worksheets for every person who reports directly to me. When I delegate a task to someone else, I just place the cursor on that task, click Cut, and then Paste the task onto the worksheet for my colleagues. In this way, I not only keep my own workload to a manageable level but also am careful about the quantity of tasks that I assign to colleagues.

At this writing, I have sixty-eight tasks on my list, with the earliest one being 104 days old—clearly ripe for pruning. Of the sixty-eight tasks, nine are A-level priorities. Every time I listen to voice mail, read incoming letters, or plan a project, the tasks go onto this master list with a new priority and date. Every morning, I highlight the tasks, then hit Data and Sort, and all of the tasks are automatically sorted in priority order. Because the spreadsheet is already installed on every computer we purchase, the extra cost for this sophisticated, automated, and effective time management system is zero. Because it is automatically backed up along with all other computer files, I can lose the computer, pour acid on the hard drive, or allow a Boston subway driver to smash it to a million pieces, and I will not endure the catastrophe suffered by someone who loses the only copy of a calendar or task list.

Linking Leadership Time Management to Student Achievement

After only a few weeks of using daily prioritized task lists in whatever manual or electronic form you choose, a picture will emerge of how you allocate your priorities, and the similarities and differences between those priorities and your organizational goals. On my list that I have shared, warts and all, seven of the top nine priorities (the A's on the current list), relate to clients, one to a publication, and one to an organizational need at the center. This probably reflects a failure to delegate as much as I should with respect to some client service matters. Only one out of nine A-level priorities is focused on internal organizational health; this conveys an exceptionally high degree of trust in my colleagues at the center (true), and it also conveys that I take some things for granted that even in an effective organization probably require greater leadership attention (also true).

What about your top priorities? If you examine your own A-level priorities, how many are related to regulatory compliance, meeting demands for reporting and information by external authorities, dealing with local personnel issues, handling parents and student complaints, and so forth? How many deal with student achievement? When I examine the task lists of many educational leaders, I rarely find a majority of the top six items directly related to student achievement. There are wonderful exceptions, such as the leader who makes it a priority to collaboratively evaluate student work with a teacher, provide feedback on student assessment, participate in professional development, or review achievement data and compare it building-level data on teaching practices and curriculum strategies.

More often than not, however, the stark evidence of the daily prioritized task list shows how rare these items are amid all the other demands on the time of an educational leader. This is not an impossible situation, and it can be reversed. It starts when, for instance, a board of education monitors its own agenda and its own demands for information from senior educational leaders. A board can ask, "How many of our information requests and other time-consuming requirements that we place on educational leaders are directly related to student achievement?" Superintendents and every central office department that generates demands for teachers and principals to complete reports can ask the same thing. Every person responsible for scheduling a meeting or professional development session can bear the same responsibility.

Articulating standards, coordinating standards, assessing standards, leading on standards, and every other activity of student achievement requires an investment of time. Without effective leadership time management, the complaints of "I don't have the time!" will drown out the voices demanding improved performance and better leadership.

Chapter Nine

Accountability

From Autopsy to Physical

Leadership Keys

The purpose of educational accountability is to improve
   student achievement
Accountability is more than test scores
Comprehensive accountability and the Leadership and
   Learning Matrix

Although it is true that the vast majority of state educational
accountability systems refer exclusively to test scores, attendance,
school safety, and the dropout rate, there is not a single school
in the nation that is prohibited from placing those numbers in
context by systematically evaluating additional variables in teaching, leadership, and curriculum. Because most accountability systems already appear to be laden with information, an educational
leader might reasonably challenge the request for yet more information and addition of elements of an accountability report that
are not required. Why, the leader asks, should we do more than is
required when we are already overburdened with accountability
systems?

The answer lies in the fundamental purpose of educational
accountability. If it is only to evaluate schools without helping leaders, teachers, and policy makers understand how to improve, then
the present system of scores and statistics serves adequately. The
present system produces convenient scores, routinely announces
the "top" and "bottom" schools, and reinforces common stereotypes

about student achievement. With a combination of superficiality and ineffectiveness, it is a nearly perfect combination of the least beneficial results for the greatest expenditure of effort. Few leaders inside or outside of educational organizations, however, find the present state of accountability tolerable. The answer is not to abandon the present system, but to improve it—and most of all, to place the data that we have in its appropriate context.

Accountability: A Physical, Not an Autopsy

Once we accept that the purpose of accountability is to improve student achievement, then the entire system of gathering and reporting accountability information can be reframed. The purpose of our efforts is not the educational version of an autopsy, in which we announce that the patient has expired and suggest some insight into the cause of death. Rather, we are concerned with the health of the patient (the patients) and thus are conducting a physical to obtain information that will improve their present and future well-being.

An autopsy is satisfied with a recitation of effects; a physical must investigate underlying causes. No pathologist, fresh from completing an autopsy, devoted much time to recommending diet, exercise, and other health regimens to the patient, as it is quite unlikely that the patient was listening. The physician conducting a physical, by contrast, devotes extensive time to understanding and communicating methods of improving health. Educational leaders are the wise physicians who must consider how to improve education, not merely how to analyze the demise of the system.

Accountability and the Leadership and Learning Matrix

Because we know that causes are essential for an understanding of improving student achievement, an accountability system that contains only test scores is inherently insufficient. An effective accountability system must integrate the principles of the Leadership and Learning Matrix introduced in Chapter Three.

Although a typical accountability system attends only to an investigation into the vertical axis of effect data, a holistic accountability system* (Reeves, 2002b) includes three distinct tiers of data analysis. The first tier includes systemwide indicators—test scores, attendance, dropout rate, safety, and other matters that apply to every school throughout the system, state, or district. The second tier of accountability indicators includes six to ten school-based indicators, measuring strategies that are uniquely suited to the needs of that school and the students it serves. These school-based indicators frequently measure teaching, curriculum, and leadership variables and thus can address the horizontal axis of the Leadership and Learning Matrix. In the context of the matrix, the horizontal axis measures the antecedents of excellence. By measuring the relationship between tier two variables (cause indicators) and tier one variables (effect indicators), a holistic accountability system gives leaders and policy makers insights into the most and least effective educational strategies. Support for implementation of these indicators is in the forms of Appendix A.

The third tier of a holistic accountability system explores the connection between the first two tiers of data using a school narrative. The third tier of the system is also a useful opportunity for the school leader to express in rich descriptive language information about the school that is not subject to quantitative analysis.

Whether or not your state or district embraces the principles of holistic accountability, each individual school leader has the opportunity to make accountability a constructive force for improving student achievement rather than an aimless exercise in reciting scores. The test of the value of the Leadership and Learning Matrix is not whether a state department of education uses it, but whether the teachers and leaders in your schools use it to improve teaching, learning, and leadership.

---

*An extensive description of holistic accountability systems, briefly addressed in this chapter, can be found in *Holistic Accountability: Serving Students, Schools, and Community* (Reeves, 2002b) and *Accountability in Action: A Blueprint for Learning Organizations* (Reeves, 2000a).

Chapter Ten

Building the Next Generation of Leaders

Leadership Keys

Identify prospective leaders

Create an educational leadership university

Invert the pyramid by supporting students, teachers, and parents

Create synergy by blending leadership, learning, and teaching

Although the national shortage of teachers has dominated educational news, an equally serious shortage of school leaders is becoming increasingly worrisome, with a number of school systems filling more than 10 percent of leadership vacancies with temporary personnel who lack administrative certification and leadership credentials. Moreover, the phenomenon of salary compression has caused a growing number of administrators to regard teaching as relatively more attractive than an administrative position; teaching salaries have increased and administrative responsibilities grown out of proportion to a relatively small increase in pay. As a result, many teachers who have achieved the top of the teaching pay scale find it difficult to accept a significant increase in workload, a decrease in job security, and an enormous increase in stress for a relatively small incremental financial gain.

Identify Prospective Leaders

In some respects, the compression issue is welcome, as it diminishes the likelihood that excellent teachers will seek an administrative job for the wrong reasons. Essentially, the leader must blend the skills of the great teacher (communicating complex ideas to a variety of audiences) with the skills of the great leader (systematically identifying and capitalizing on strengths within the organization to achieve extraordinary goals).

Most school systems are far better served by identifying and developing leaders from among their own colleagues than by hiring from other systems or relying exclusively upon the leadership preparation program of a local university. Moreover, schools must create a low-risk way for a prospective leader to pursue an internship, gain leadership experience, and confront the possibility that the path of leadership does not suit the person. We dare not lose excellent classroom teachers because a leadership position once sought is no longer attractive to the candidate, or the candidate is no longer needed by the district.

In addition to developing prospective leaders among the teaching ranks, a school system should also identify leaders from a growing number of second-career educators, notably those with military, business, and nonprofit organizational experience. No resume entry, however, can replace the realistic scenario afforded by a leadership development program in which the prospective leader must deal with real students, parents, and teachers daily and then reflect on those experiences systematically. Whereas traditional leadership programs react to theoretical case studies, the new wave of leadership development program writes its own case studies, implementing real decisions and reflecting on actual successes and errors.

By considering a leadership training program as an investment in the future, the school system has a chance to reconsider the traditional method of evaluating, recruiting, and training principals and other leaders. A growing number of programs that blend real-world experience with academic reading and research and reflection among professional colleagues are replacing traditional approaches that rely upon an accumulation of credit hours, superficially distributed among finance, testing, and personnel but promoting readiness for actual leadership responsibility in none of those areas.

The essential question that these districts must face is, "What are the knowledge and skills that school leaders in this system need to be successful?" Furthermore, these districts must ask, "How will we know when a candidate possesses the essential knowledge and skills required for leadership success?" A portfolio of actual leadership decisions (including analysis of alternatives, the process of decision making, and the results of actual decisions) is likely to be much more revealing than the traditional contents of a transcript of grades in leadership classes.

Create an Educational Leadership University

Another way to expand the pool of leadership candidates is to completely transform professional development for leaders. The school system could become a center of leadership training, providing skills in personnel management, strategic planning, and data analysis that are needed by all leaders. Just as leading corporations have established their own university-level training centers for leadership development, a school system can and must do the same, inviting not only candidates from its own district but educators, business people, and employees of government and nonprofit organizations to participate (for a fee, of course) in the district-sponsored leadership training.

Just as the Harvard Business School is training leaders in politics, nonprofit organizations, and education, your leadership training institute can offer valuable insight, knowledge, and skills to business leaders. More importantly, with each cadre of leaders that you train you find potential candidates for your own leadership team. By making this a university-level endeavor with university credit, you can also integrate the training of educators and leaders into the university curriculum to a much greater extent than is now typically the case.

Transforming the Leadership Training Curriculum

Leadership training at the university level generally includes courses in school finance; education law; personnel management;

and a blend of research, assessment, and statistics. Though a few leadership curriculum designs are changing to encompass reflection on actual leadership experience, the more common curriculum is in place because it reflects state certification requirements; this sort of training is a ticket to be punched rather than an indicator of leadership readiness and preparation.

There is a better way. A school system or group of school systems, organized by the county, region, or state, could create a "senior leadership institute." In the institute format, participants engage in a combination of research, case study, small group work, and personal reflection. Rather than the fragmented curriculum that dominates most leadership programs, an effective senior leadership institute should focus on four key areas: people, strategies, organizations, and systems.

People

Goleman (1998, 2002) has made clear that the so-called soft skills have a hard impact on organizational performance. Moreover, his research strongly suggests that neither intelligence nor analytical ability separated the most successful leaders from those who were merely average. The distinguishing features were self-awareness, empathy, social awareness, and social skills—all part of what he described as emotional intelligence. Contrary to the notion that these skills are ingrained, he demonstrates that emotional intelligence and the behavior associated with it can be acquired and practiced. Whereas most courses in personnel management focus on the legal and technical issues of evaluation, correction, and compliance, those are but a small part of the skills necessary to lead a complex organization.

Strategies

Robert Kaplan, of the Harvard Business school, co-creator of "the balanced scorecard," has made the same case in business that I have made in education: accountability is more than a single number, whether it is earnings or test scores. Kaplan and his colleague, David Norton (2001), have examined strategies of organizations outside the business world and found that most of them are distinguished only by their girth. They include "lists of programs and initiatives, not the outcomes the organization is trying to achieve. These organizations must understand . . . that strategy is not only what the organization intends to do, but also what it decides not to do—a message that is particularly relevant for nonprofits and government departments" (p. 133).

The essence of successful strategy is not creation of a planning document, but execution of strategy and continuous evaluation of the information related to decisions. Throughout this process of execution and evaluation, leaders are incessantly comparing the mission and vision with the decisions made throughout the organization. Strategy, in brief, gives the leader the context of each decision. As Kaplan and Norton (2001) have both suggested, an essential part of this kind of strategy is deciding what not to do, not merely assembling projects, tasks, and wish lists. The senior leadership institute is an ideal opportunity for participants to examine strategy, challenge its foundation, research the connection (or lack of it) between data and decisions, and reevaluate the mission as an effective filter for decision making.

Organizations

Paul Houston (personal interview, Mar. 28, 2002) notes that in a growing number of school districts the central office is undergoing fundamental reorganization. Although the very mention of central office reorganization may be political suicide for a prospective school leader, a senior leadership institute offers a safe environment in which the *what if?* questions can be safely raised. Once the concept of a chief academic officer has been established, there are profound implications for the central office. Rather than have technology in the business office, where it usually resides, it might be moved to an academic department. The same is true of personnel, a department often (and wisely) separated on the organization chart from the academic leadership of the district. In the senior leadership institute, participants explore organizations, staffing patterns, and position descriptions. An essential part of executing strategy is effective creation, destruction, and re-creation of organizational structure.

Systems

Understanding systems is not merely repetition of organizational structure, as is commonly assumed. It is a way of recognizing the relationships in all the work and results of an organization. As Senge (1990) defines it: "Systems thinking makes understanding the subtlest aspect of the learning organization—the new way individuals perceive themselves and their world. At the heart of a learning organization is a shift of mind—from seeing ourselves as separate from the world to connected to the world, from seeing problems as caused by someone or something 'out there' to seeing how our own actions create the problems we experience. A learning organization is a place where people are continually discovering how they create their reality. And how they can change it" (pp. 12–13).

Because building a learning organization depends on a leader who understands, models, and practices systems thinking, it is one of the four core components of the senior leadership institute.

If you choose to build a senior leadership institute, be prepared for the kitchen sink syndrome, in which everyone's good idea, favorite speaker, latest book, and state mandate finds its way into the curriculum. Doing that, you only re-create what already exists, with a little more superficiality. If, by contrast, you remain focused on the four key areas of people, strategies, organization, and systems, you produce leaders who think deeply about their present and future positions and about your organization. If they are uncomfortable with such a challenge, you are far better off to know it during a leadership institute than after a few months on the job.

A final essential part of a successful senior leadership institute is one-to-one coaching and a peer network. The institute is not merely a collection of classes but the core of your learning organization, in which discussion, learning, confrontation, and reaction in the period between official courses are at least as important as the class meetings. Ideally, these intersession activities include personal coaching by faculty members and a lively dialogue on focused topics of discussion. A successful senior leadership institute class creates a document of leadership experiences that directly relate the learning of the institute to the daily lives of the participants. These collected experiences should be published and widely shared in your organization.

Inverting the Pyramid: Supporting Students, Teachers, and Parents

Although the effective leader enjoys the challenge of motivating other people, perhaps the worst reason for someone to pursue a career in educational leadership is the fantasy that a leader is able to control other people. In fact, the most effective leaders routinely serve others, namely, the employees and other stakeholders.

As a young military officer, I joined other commanders in following the British tradition in which the officers ate last at every meal and on several holidays during the year served the troops as well. To this day, I have seen leaders of very large school systems make a point of picking up a stray piece of paper, making the point that cleanliness is a value practiced by everyone, including the top leaders of the organization. Similarly, I have witnessed leaders of schools with enrollment approaching four thousand students take the time to evaluate student work. In those districts, the example is set by superintendents who routinely work with students (including many who teach a regular class several times a week), counsel teachers, and pay attention to the family as well as professional needs of employees.

I have previously written about Stan Scheer, who, as a principal, assistant superintendent, and superintendent, regularly puts
himself on the substitute teacher list, spending half-days and full
days in the classroom, enduring the confusion and bewilderment
faced by substitute teachers every day. It is no accident that this
same empathic and demanding leader takes donuts and coffee to
the bus drivers at five in the morning and personally thanks the
cafeteria staff for their rarely noticed efforts. When he expects
great things from his staff, everyone knows that he asks no more
of any employee in the district than he regularly demands of
himself.

Mary Ann Dewann, an exceptionally effective principal in
Wayne Township near Indianapolis, personally meets with every
student in the fourth, fifth, and sixth grades to discuss their progress
and personally administers buildingwide writing and mathematics assessments in classes regularly. One urban principal gave up his
office so it could become the parents' welcome lounge, while
another principal in a high-mobility school turned her office into a
student welcome center to create a quiet, warm, and friendly place
for the steady stream of new students and parents coming to the
school.

The list of principals, from new leaders to veterans of many
decades, who invert the pyramid and exemplify the traits of ser-
vant leadership is a long one, but the actions of these leaders continue to attract notice because they are an exception. There are,
unfortunately, many other leaders and prospective leaders who
attempt to reign by decree, replacing collaboration with dic-
tates and displacing trust with suspicion. What is particularly
alarming are the school leaders I see who do not appear to like children and, for that matter, do not enjoy being in a classroom. They
handle themselves well at the Rotary Club or school board meeting, but they studiously avoid schools, particularly during the time
when students are passing in the hallway or parents might be con-
gregated in the waiting area.

Identifying the Next Generation of Leaders

It is clear, then, that there is a crisis in school leadership. No matter how many books we publish on the subject, no matter how lofty our aims, no matter how good leadership training opportunities may be, all efforts are for naught if we do not have school leaders. In the nation's largest school system, New York City, two-thirds of principals have less than five years of experience and more than a third of them do not even have two years' experience. Twelve percent of the city's schools opened last school year without a permanent principal (Holloway, 2001). The situation is not limited to New York; Senator John Kerry described the national shortage of principals as a desperate situation, with 40 percent of principals nationally expected to retire within ten years (Stricherz, 2001).

At the senior leadership level, the situation is worse, with superintendent positions unfilled. Compensation packages worth hundreds of thousands of dollars (the superintendent in Dallas now earns in excess of $300,000 annually) have not been sufficient to reduce the rate at which system-level leaders are fired, or simply burn out. Some of this chaos is self-imposed, as changing board priorities lead to a revolving door in the superintendent's office. Other causes are external; CEO compensation has skyrocketed elsewhere in the economy, creating incentives for many people with leadership talent to seek employment outside of education.

The Accelerating Path to Leadership

The traditional path of school leadership typically meant progression from teaching to the administrative ranks, followed by a stint as an assistant principal, and ultimately as a school leader. Prior to assuming leadership of a school, the principal enjoyed multiple leadership opportunities, from leading a task force or committee to chairing a parent-teacher group or assuming leadership responsibility in a community organization. During this time, the prospective principal could develop mentoring relationships with other leaders, study the leadership literature, and reflect on the necessary move from theory to reality as a school leader.

Although the first year of the principal is always challenging, a person with such extended preparation faced challenges that could be anticipated yet tapped into a reservoir of information and contacts as each new challenge arose. Now that path is accelerated, with people whose experience in teaching is brief, whose administrative training consisted of weekend and evening classes crammed into an already overloaded schedule, and who have had little or no leadership experience prior to assuming real leadership responsibility. For a teacher serving as an acting principal, there is even less preparation, with the district relying on good judgment and common sense—two qualities that are needed, to be sure, but that alone are insufficient to prepare a leader for the variety of responsibilities faced by today's school leader.

At the superintendent level, some boards are turning to leaders from the military, business, political, and nonprofit arenas to satisfy their leadership needs. An active core of retired superintendents have found employment as a contracted acting superintendent for a district that has not been able to find a candidate to fill the job. An acting superintendent meets a temporary need, but short tenure ensures that, on a national level, continuity of policy is unlikely. Moreover, when a new system leader announces changes, a strong undercurrent of cynicism remains that says, "I've outlasted three other superintendents with new ideas, and I'll outlast this one too."

The Chief Academic Officer

To identify the next generation of leaders, we must cast a wide net, finding people who display potential for organizational leadership and for instructional leadership.

The ranks of potential leaders are deeper than we think. One reason the shortage of principals has been so acute is, quite simply, that we have not asked enough people if they are interested in educational leadership. Buckingham and Coffman (1999) note that one of the most distinctive characteristics of an effective organization is that employees discuss their progress, development, and future with someone in the organization at least every six months.

The two qualities are not necessarily found in the same person; hence a growing number of school systems are identifying both a chief operating officer and a chief academic officer. One of them might also hold the title of superintendent and thus report directly to the board and be the chief executive officer of the district.

Once we acknowledge the need to differentiate these senior leadership positions, the pool of potential leadership candidates becomes significantly larger. Teachers with an interest in instructional leadership can aspire to become a chief academic officer and not be limited in their career advancement by failing to master the intricacies of school finance. Leaders whose experience is primarily in the business, military, or nonprofit sector can aspire to system-level leadership despite the paucity of their experience in curriculum and assessment. Their skills in community relations, technology, and organizational development are also vital for a community. The essential strategy must be identifying not a single pool of ideal leaders but rather a pool of leaders with complementary strengths.

One thing that all leaders in the pool have in common is acute understanding of their own limitations and of their need to have other leaders by their side, each with his or her own set of skills and abilities. This is the opposite of the Lone Ranger model of leadership that has dominated the business scene and, to some extent, been replicated in school districts. Sergiovanni (2000) makes the case powerfully that the charisma of the leader who dominates the organization by sheer force of personality might be counterproductive, as sustaining the organization becomes a matter of the personality of an individual rather than quality of ideas. Thus the new generation of leaders must combine the necessary focus and passion (typically associated with the individual leader) with the humility and accurate self-assessment necessary for today's team leader.

Contrast this standard with the typical educational system in which teachers are evaluated annually for a few years, but after tenure rarely evaluated at all. Those evaluations are almost always retrospective, limited to a form created by collective bargaining, and thus not oriented to what leadership positions the teacher might consider in the future. Building administrators and central office administrators are evaluated at best annually; many of the evaluations I have reviewed are stunningly consistent, with phrases that appear to be taken from a computer program. They attempt to evaluate performance but rarely consider the future impact.

When someone has an interest in potential leadership, then professional development opportunities can be afforded them that expose the person to leadership training; internships can be used for short-term leadership experience. All this can be designed to let both the organization and the prospective leader gain experience and background before turning inexorably to a new career path. The majority of teachers, for example, do not want to become administrators. But there are surely more teachers with leadership potential than are now being identified. The same is true in the counseling office, nurses office, media center, and central service department.

Create Synergy by Blending Leadership, Learning, and Teaching

When was the last time your superintendent or other educational leader led a class? I don't mean reading aloud before the cameras or giving a speech to a school assembly. I mean teaching a lesson, motivating students, assessing for learning, making on-the-spot decisions for reteaching, assessing again, and creating the spark of life we call learning. When was the last time a leadership meeting felt like your best seminar in college? The seminar leader asks probing questions and the well-prepared participants make lively and informed contributions. You leave the meeting feeling that you have learned so much and knowing at the same time that you have much yet to learn. You feel you have made a significant contribution but also developed a healthy respect for your colleagues, who surprise you with their insight, analysis, and background information.

If it has been too long since those ideals were part of your organization, then take heart. It is not impossible. The synergy between leadership and learning is so powerful, so important, that it cannot be overlooked. Developing a new generation of leaders demands that our best teachers lead and that our best leaders teach. If each staff meeting is regarded as an opportunity to model the very best in teaching and learning, there will be fewer meetings, each much richer in content and more productive in results. A few guidelines can start to produce this synergy. For each meeting, the leader should ask:

- What do I expect the participants of this meeting to know and be able to do as a result of it? In other words, what are the standards that participants will meet as a result of this? If the answer is, "Nothing; it's just for information," then a meeting is unnecessary. Send them a memo.
- How will I know if the participants in the meeting have met the standards? If the answer is, "They'll nod their heads in meek acquiescence," then the meeting is a waste of time. Standards without assessment are as impotent in the board room as they are in the classroom.
- Will this standard contribute to our core mission? Does it meet the criteria for a power standard because it is enduring, has leverage, and is essential for the next level of learning? If not, it may be a nice idea, but you just don't have time for it. Focus on the essentials.

The next generation of leaders may not be represented by the resumes in the file of administrative applicants. A member of the next generation of leaders may be the quiet person in your next meeting who has not spoken up because you have not asked a question. It may be the kindergarten teacher brimming with confidence, intelligence, empathy, and enthusiasm, who has never been asked, "Would you consider learning more about school leadership?" It may be a community leader or business manager who has been active in school affairs and is seeking deep meaning in a second career. To develop the next generation of school leaders, you must create a wider pool of applicants and take personal responsibility for training that pool. Without the action of today's school leaders, the present crisis in school leadership will threaten every other achievement for which you have worked so hard.

Leadership Reflections

1. How deep is your leadership bench? Specifically, how many people in your organization are now qualified to be superintendent? How many are qualified to occupy a senior position in the central office? How many are qualified to be a building principal?

2. Look at the last ten people hired for a leadership position in your organization. Where did they come from? Inside or outside the organization? What were the patterns that you noticed about their background? On the basis of those observations, are these sources of leadership talent sufficient for the next five years?

3. List the requirements in your area to receive certification for educational leadership. For each requirement, identify the core area (people, strategies, organization, systems) into which the official requirement could fit. What do you notice about this method of organizing the required curriculum? Are some areas overrepresented? Are some of the core areas not represented at all in the required courses?

4. If you have been a teacher, what is the subject that you most love to teach? Could you arrange to teach it again, even if for only two or three hours a week? If you have never been a teacher, what is a subject that you would love to teach? Could you arrange to teach it, perhaps in partnership with an experienced teacher, for two or three hours a week? If you do this, arrange for monthly meetings among other leaders who are spending some time teaching. How do the observations that leaders make in the classroom relate to the observations made by full-time educators?

Chapter Eleven: Conclusion

The Enduring Values of the Leader

The Key to Surviving the Disappointments and Disasters of the Leadership Life

Leadership Keys

Values endure; procedures do not

Find your enduring values

Decide what's worth fighting for

It is most revealing to have a conversation with a committed professional and hear his or her reflections on persisting in the face of disappointment. Why do police officers stay on the force even when bad guys get away? Why do physicians and nurses return to work even when death and illnesses are senseless and unpredictable?

Why do teachers return to the classroom even when students are sometimes unmotivated and belligerent? One teacher explained her reason for maintaining student portfolios by noting:

> On my worst day, when I question my value to this profession, I can take out any portfolio and see the dramatic progress that students make while they are with me. For some students, this is a period of four years, starting in the ninth grade when they were confused and barely able to compose a coherent paragraph, and continuing through their senior year as I glimpse a copy of their college application essays. In a matter of seconds, I remind myself what a profound difference I make in the lives of these students, even on those days when I barely am able to recognize it.

The value that sustained this wonderful educator was not a policy about portfolios or a procedure related to writing standards, but her bone-deep belief in the potential of her students and her conviction that her personal and professional efforts opened doors that made a life-changing difference for every student.

Find Your Enduring Values

Just as I have never heard a teacher remark that the source of enduring inspiration was "Standard 34.2," I have never heard a school leader cite a policy, procedure, or standard as a source of resilience and endurance. Rather, there are deep values that rarely appear in administrative discussion, board minutes, a staff development agenda, or leadership memorandum. As I cast my eye around the offices of the most successful leaders I know, a few clues emerge. Sometimes it is insertion of a favorite book of children's stories or poems amid the tomes on leadership and educational policy, making clear that the delight in words and fantasy has not been diminished by years or by advanced degrees. At other times it is the pictures, not only of families or congratulatory handshakes with public officials, but photos taken with students and colleagues, reflecting a lifetime of changing tie width, dress length, and hairstyle, but not one iota of change in commitment to and love for students and learning.

Take a moment to consider what your enduring values are. These are the values that would pass this test: suppose that on this very day, you learn that your school will be shut down, your job will be eliminated, and you will be on the street, perhaps working again in education and perhaps finding a totally different line of work just to make ends meet. Which beliefs will be unchanged by such a series of challenging events?

The tragic events of September 11, 2001, give the world some insight into these enduring values. The conventional wisdom in the aftermath of these tragedies was dominated by speculation about how the world has changed forever, but the more stunning revelation is about what has endured. As I have spoken with educators from New York and around the world, their optimism, resilience, and confidence in children and teachers remain unshakable. Buildings crumble, but courage, decency, and respect are values transcending even the events that are literally and figuratively earth-shattering. As this book goes to press, the *New York Times* continues to publish its regular feature entitled "Portraits of Grief." As heartbreaking as each story is—recounting the death of a bride of thirty days, of a gallant firefighter, of a family of three including a two-and-a-half-year-old child—each story also contains clues into the quest for enduring values.

The stories of thousands of victims tell of little league coaches, volunteer tutors, parents, and children. What is striking is how familiar and ordinary these victims were, making clear that the cross-section of people from American and several other nations who were lost on that tragic day is also a representation of what remains. The happy brides, gallant firefighters, tutors, parents, teachers, and children who still walk among us remind us of what was lost, and also of what endures. Another tragedy of the past few years, the murders at Columbine High School in Colorado, similarly showed a nation how a teacher could literally lay down his life for his students, and how a school and community could rebuild from unbearable grief.

Some people may believe that values are intrinsic, cosmically woven into the psyche of each human in a way we cannot understand, but those committed to the principles of leadership and learning must surely believe that our values can be shaped, informed, and molded not only by our heritage but by the events around us. These reflections give each leader the opportunity to create a personal leadership credo, expressing beliefs that go far beyond the platitudes of the day and identify those few values that are worthy of our commitment of heart and mind. Once these enduring values and beliefs have been established, the door is open to contemplation and discussion of a variety of alternatives. If you came to this book committed to educational standards, or if this book has perhaps influenced you in that direction, then you may wish to consider this statement as a starting point for your own credo:

I believe in fairness, because the value of my work as an educator depends not only on success but on justice. Therefore I will fight for fairness, even when it is inconvenient and unpopular, even when it messes up the schedule and challenges traditional assumptions, even when it draws students, parents, and teachers far outside of their comfort zone. Because I have decided to fight for fairness, it means that I must fight against grading practices, assessment techniques, and accountability systems that compare students to moving targets or to one another, and demand systems that compare student performance to a fair and consistent set of standards.

I believe in respect for the individual potential of every human, because the value of my work as an educator is not defined by the past experiences and opportunities of my students, but by the experiences and opportunities that my colleagues and I create. Because I have decided to fight for individual respect, it means that I must fight against any curriculum, schedule, teaching technique, or assessment regimen that cares more about where my students start than how they finish. This will influence everything from how we grade a single paper to the calculation of final grades to the manner in which student work is communicated to parents and the community. Just as I respect the human potential of every student, I believe in the potential of every faculty member, including those only days from retirement, to grow and learn and improve every day. I model that commitment to lifelong learning, pursuing new knowledge and being vulnerable to the mistakes of the novice on a regular basis.

I believe in collaboration, because I am acutely aware of my own limitations and those of any other individual. But as surely as I acknowledge individual limitations, I am convinced of the extraordinary potential of the success of a committed group with shared values, enthusiasm, optimism, and commitment. If I fight for collaboration, it means that I must fight against isolationism and indifference. Ours is an inherently collaborative profession, and my respect for individual creativity does not reduce my demand for consensus on the essentials. Indeed, my commitment to fairness for students requires that educational opportunities, teacher expectations, and classroom assessment practices are never a matter of luck but a matter of right.

Fairness, respect, and collaboration. It's a start, and some of these concepts, probably expressed differently, might begin your own leadership credo. At the end of the day, neither students nor other stakeholders will ask how many levels were on your performance assessment rubric, how many standards you had, nor the type of regression coefficient you used on your leadership matrix. They will only ask what you believed so strongly that you found it worthy of your will to fight.

Three Paths of Leadership: Pyrrhus, Icarus, and Ulysses

Three Greek characters, one historical and two mythological, offer a composite glimpse of the leadership path. None of them paints the picture of the illusory leader who, using wit and superior strength, resolves every crisis and rides into the sunset at the end of every episode. In fact, all three are flawed characters, but each informs our view of leadership, and ultimately of ourselves. King Pyrrhus, from whose name arises the term *Pyrrhic victory*, committed so many resources to a successful battle that he jeopardized his kingdom. "One more such victory," he sadly remarked, "and we are undone." Icarus, of course, flew higher and higher on his magical wings until, caught up in his hubris and sense of invincibility, he soared too close to the sun and, wings melted, plummeted to earth. Ulysses' journey continued for two decades, while he resisted the call of Sirens, navigated treacherous waters, and endured endless betrayals and disappointment at every turn. We remember him not merely for success but for endurance on the journey and resilience in the face of repeated disappointments. He completed his journey weary and wounded, but confident that the goal he set twenty years earlier was always before him.

The women and men who lead schools, educational systems, and national policy can be easily tempted by the impetuousness of Pyrrhus or the vanity of Icarus. Let us hope that most of them are guided by the dogged determination of Ulysses and given a journey that is neither easy nor universally satisfying, but a journey in which the leader never forgets the primary purpose of the journey. Let us further hope that the guide for these leaders on the journey is not the siren call of conventional wisdom, but the beacon of their enduring values.

Appendix A
Leadership Tools, Checklists, and Forms

A note about reproducible forms: purchasers of this book are granted the authority to copy and use the forms in this Appendix for educational use within their school or district. This authority for reproduction is limited by the following stipulations:

- All forms must be reproduced in full, including the copyright notice and the stipulation that reproduction is limited for educational and noncommercial use.

- Reproduction is explicitly not authorized for commercial use, including resale of these forms or packaging of these forms into professional development handouts that are sold or marketed by any other entity, whether commercial, nonprofit, or educational.

Forms in This Appendix

A.1 Student Achievement Form
A.2 Educational Practice Form
A.3 Leadership Practice Form
A.4 Curriculum Practice Form
A.5 Data Analysis: Ordered Pairs Linking Professional Practice to Student Achievement
A.6 Worksheet: Leadership and Learning Matrix Data
A.7 Personal Leadership and Learning Matrix

A.8   Professional Practice Inventory

A.9   Leadership Practice Inventory

A.10 Curriculum Practice Inventory

A.11 Factors Influencing Student Achievement, Not Controllable by Leader

A.12 Factors Influencing Student Achievement, Subject to Influence by Leader

A.13 Parent Communication Checklist

A.14 Faculty Communication Checklist

A.15 Community Communication Checklist

A.16 Classroom Checklist for Standards Implementation

A.17 School Checklist for Standards Implementation

A.18 District Checklist for Standards Implementation

A.1. Student Achievement Form

Achievement indicator: _____

Data source: _____

Date of administration: _____

Class	Indicator	Result (Percentage Proficient or Higher)

A.2. Educational Practice Form

Practice: _____

Data source: _____

Date: _____

Class	Indicator	Measurement (Frequency, Percentage, Etc.)

A.3. Leadership Practice Form

Leadership practice: _____

Data source: _____

Date: _____

Class	Indicator	Measurement (Frequency, Percentage, Etc.)

A.4. Curriculum Practice Form

Practice: _____

Data source: _____

Date: _____

Class	Indicator	Measurement (Frequency, Percentage, Etc.)

A.5. Data Analysis: Ordered Pairs Linking Professional Practice to Student Achievement

Professional Practice	Measurement (Horizontal Axis)	Achievement Variable	Measurement (Vertical Axis)

A.6. Worksheet: Leadership and Learning Matrix Data

Antecedent of Excellence	Relationship to Student Achievement (R^2, Correlation Coefficient, or Other Indicator of Relationship Between Cause and Effect Variables)	Student Results Indicators	Percentage of Students Proficient or Higher, Using Scale of 0 to 100%

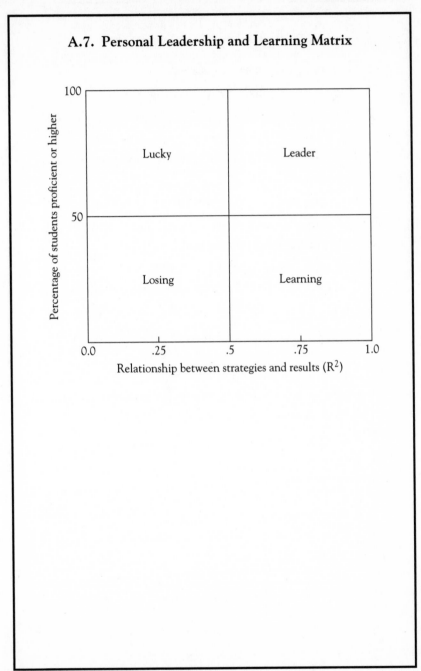

A.7. **Personal Leadership and Learning Matrix**

A.8. Professional Practice Inventory

☐ Frequency of writing assessment

☐ Frequency of collaborative scoring

☐ Percentage of agreement on scoring of anonymous student work

☐ Time required to reach 80 percent consensus in scoring

☐ Percentage of lessons integrating technology

☐ Percentage of non–language-arts lessons involving student writing with editing and rewriting

☐ Frequency of feedback to students that resulted in direct action by students based on that feedback

☐ Frequency of updates in student writing portfolio

☐ Frequency of updates in student reading assessment (Running Record or similar folder)

☐ Percentage of student portfolios in _____ (name of academic subject) receiving comparable evaluations by colleague or administrator

☐ _____

☐ _____

☐ _____

☐ _____

☐ _____

☐ _____

☐ _____

☐ _____

☐ _____

☐ _____

A.9. Leadership Practice Inventory

☐ Percentage of faculty meeting discussion and action items relating to student achievement

☐ Percentage of professional development activities directly related to classroom practice supporting student achievement

☐ Percentage of parents who agree or strongly agree with the statement, "I feel welcome to visit my child's classroom at any time."

☐ Frequency of recognition of teacher best practices

☐ Percentage of A-level tasks on daily prioritized task list directly related to improved student achievement

☐ Percentage of faculty members with student achievement practices in assessment, curriculum, and instruction at the "distinguished" level according to a collaboratively scored rubric of professional practices

☐ Percentage of available time by certified staff members devoted to student contact

☐ Percentage of students with identified academic deficiency who are rescheduled for additional assistance within thirty days of the identified need

☐ Percentage of leader-initiated parent contacts related to academic achievement

☐ _____

☐ _____

☐ _____

☐ _____

☐ _____

☐ _____

A.10. Curriculum Practice Inventory

☐ Percentage of students who are one or more grade levels below current grade in reading who receive targeted assistance

☐ Percentage of classrooms that allow multiple opportunities for student success

☐ Percentage of failing finals that were subject to resubmission and potential success

☐ Percentage of students participating in advanced classes

☐ Percentage of students participating in "preadvanced" classes

☐ Percentage of leader visits in which the actual activity corresponds to the planned activity

☐ Percentage of physical education classes incorporating academic content and assessment in writing, reading, mathematics, or science

☐ Percentage of music classes incorporating academic content and assessment in writing, reading, mathematics, or social studies

☐ Percentage of art classes incorporating academic content and assessment in writing, reading, mathematics, science, or social studies

☐ _____

☐ _____

☐ _____

☐ _____

☐ _____

☐ _____

☐ _____

☐ _____

A.11. Factors Influencing Student Achievement, Not Controllable by Leader

Factor	Student	Family	Environment/ Other

A.12. Factors Influencing Student Achievement, Subject to Influence by Leader

Factor	Teaching	Curriculum	Leadership

A.13. Parent Communication Checklist

Multiple channels of parent communication are available:

- ☐ Face-to-face meetings at school
- ☐ Personal meetings at nonschool locations, including

  _____

- ☐ Incoming phone calls with personal response
- ☐ Incoming phone calls with voice mail
- ☐ School-initiated calls by teachers
- ☐ School-initiated calls by administrators
- ☐ School-initiated calls by other student advocates
- ☐ Internet-based communication
- ☐ E-mail initiated by parents
- ☐ E-mail initiated by school
- ☐ Other channels of communication:
- ☐ _____
- ☐ _____
- ☐ _____
- ☐ Student achievement results are communicated to parents with more information than letter grades.
- ☐ Student achievement results for students in danger of failure are communicated at least every week to parents.
- ☐ Student achievement results for students previously in danger of failure who are now demonstrating exceptional progress are communicated at least every week to parents.

- ☐ Teachers identify a watch list of students in danger of failure; a team approach, including parents, is used to monitor and improve student performance.
- ☐ Parents have multiple ways of becoming engaged in school support activities.
- ☐ More than 90 percent of students have a caring adult who is regularly involved in school support activities.
- ☐ Parents have the opportunity to participate in scoring student work using standards and scoring guides.
- ☐ Parent scoring of student work is comparable to teacher scoring of student work.
- ☐ Test information is sent to parents in a timely and understandable form.

- ☐ _____
- ☐ _____
- ☐ _____
- ☐ _____
- ☐ _____
- ☐ _____
- ☐ _____
- ☐ _____
- ☐ _____
- ☐ _____
- ☐ _____

A.14. Faculty Communication Checklist

☐ The primary method for faculty announcements is a written or e-mailed list, not a verbal announcement in a meeting or during classroom time.

☐ The focus of faculty communication in faculty meetings, grade-level meetings, and departmental meetings is achievement of a professional consensus on the meaning of *proficient* in student work.

☐ The degree of faculty consensus on student proficiency is regularly monitored and posted.

☐ If the level of faculty consensus is below 80 percent, special leadership attention is devoted to improving scoring guides, reducing ambiguity, and increasing clarity until the 80 percent consensus level is restored.

☐ Schedules are set in such a way that, even for final examinations, faculty members have time to collaboratively score student work, communicate with students, and allow students to respect faculty feedback as well as improve the quality of their own work.

☐ Faculty members are clearly and specifically authorized to change schedules and lesson plans to assist students in meeting the requirements of academic content standards.

☐ Faculty members are clearly and specifically authorized to reduce curriculum content to focus on the most important "power standards" and essential skills.

☐ Faculty members regularly share best practices, documenting specific successful practices. Aside from collaborative evaluation of real student work, this documentation and sharing of best practices is the dominant feature of faculty meetings and professional development sessions.

☐ Faculty members personally lead professional development sessions for this building and for other buildings.

☐ Faculty members routinely collaborate with staff from other buildings, including grade levels above and below their current grade level.

☐ The results of schoolwide and districtwide common end-of-course and end-of-grade level assessments are published, discussed, and used to inform future practice.

A.15. Community Communication Checklist

☐ The community receives a comprehensive accountability report, including student achievement indicators as well as the "antecedents of excellence"
involving teaching,
leadership, and curriculum variables.

☐ Community communications include monthly success stories from schools featuring specific teachers
and students.

☐ Community communications include multiple
channels:

Speaker's bureau of teachers, administrators, students,
and parents

News releases

Publications created by students

Publications created by teachers and leaders

Television or radio broadcasts

Internet-based communications (Website and e-mail)

☐ Community members who have young children due to
enter a local school in the future are invited to parent
activities.

☐ Community members with children in home school
and private school are invited to parent activities.

☐ Political leaders, business leaders, and community
leaders are regularly invited for two-way exchange
with faculty members, leaders, students, and parents.

☐ Student academic success is showcased in the school's most prominent display areas (trophy cases, hallways, and so on).

☐ The school recognizes student academic success with the same intensity with which the community recognizes athletic success.

☐ _____

☐ _____

☐ _____

☐ _____

☐ _____

☐ _____

A.16. Classroom Checklist for Standards Implementation

☐ **Standards are highly visible in the classroom.** This need not imply every standard related to that grade level or subject, but it certainly must include the standards that are being addressed in the class during the current week. Students have a right to understand the expectations they are to meet, and teachers have a right to understand the parameters within which their instruction takes place. This serves not only to focus students and teachers but also as an antidote to administrators and policy makers who are sometimes tempted to suggest extras for the classroom. To put a fine point on it, school leaders must think twice before taking a good idea (such as character education) and transforming it into an additional curriculum in the school day. Teachers can reasonably ask, "Which standard on this wall shall I take down in order to make room for the new requirements?" The same is true for myriad curriculum requirements that, by themselves, seemed innocent but taken together form a mountain of time requirements for classroom instruction that inevitably compete with academic content standards. Examples commonly heard are the obvious ones of character education and drug, alcohol, and tobacco education, but also newly established mandatory curricula: sensitivity training, bully-proofing, diversity training, free enterprise education, sexual orientation tolerance training. There are a host of other items requiring curriculum documents, assemblies, and even assessments. When these ideas are implemented as part of a curriculum in critical thinking, social studies, or health education, that is one thing. If they have the practical impact of reducing the amount of reading and writing in a classroom and overall reducing the focus on achievement of academic standards, then leaders must confront the divergence between their principles (which are based on the value of fairness and the practice of standards-based education) and the reality of a fragmented day in which some students succeed, some fail, and teachers frantically bounce from one curriculum area to another like a pinball in a poorly leveled machine.

☐ **The standards are expressed in student-accessible language.** A few states, such as Illinois, have taken the time to express some of their standards in language that makes sense to students—and, for that matter, to parents not immersed in the jargon of standards. The work of most states, however, can be charitably described as the result of the effort of a very earnest committee. Membership in this committee typically excludes fourth graders, and as a result the wording of the standard not only eludes our students but also strikes their parents as obscure. The remedy for this problem is not to complain about standards, but to add value to the standards by restating them in language that is clear and accessible to all students. There is ample precedent for this. Teachers do not put the state criminal statutes on a poster at the front of the room, nor do they display the local board of education disciplinary code. Instead, they display the class rules, using language that students, parents, and teachers alike can understand. This should be the model for expressing standards and expectations for student academic proficiency.

☐ **Examples of proficient and exemplary student work are displayed throughout the classroom.** In some schools, this is called the "wall of fame," on which the work of present and former students is displayed. Some schools even use the trophy case for this purpose, making it clear to parents and visitors that student achievement is valued and that students in this school have already demonstrated success is possible. Some of these displays do not include student names; the purpose is not to elevate one student over another but rather to give a model to all students of what successful writing, mathematics, science, or social studies work looks like. Success in these schools is never a mystery. Displaying student work clearly links the standards to real student work. These displays have the added advantage of allowing school leaders to check that each classroom has the same level of quality expectation, and that expectations for student proficiency are always linked to the standard rather than to idiosyncratic judgment about a student.

☐ **For every assignment, the teacher publishes in advance the explicit expectations for proficient student work.** Although a full scoring guide may not always be necessary, it is absolutely essential that students enter every academic activity knowing in advance what success means. They need not guess, nor must they merely attempt to beat other students. They know precisely what is expected, whether through a rubric, checklist, or other document that clearly establishes the rules of the assignment.

☐ **Student evaluation is always done according to the standards and scoring guide, and never on the curve.** When I ask students, "How did you get that grade?" I frequently hear the honest reply, "I don't know." In a standards-based classroom, this is never the case. The rationale for grading is not the mysterious judgment of the teacher, but a reflection of a scoring guide that is based upon a clear set of standards.

☐ **The teacher can explain to any parent or other stakeholder the specific expectations of students for the year.** Parents must be able to ask, "What does my child need to know and be able to do in order to be successful this year?" They should receive an answer that is consistent and coherent. Although the initial impulse to reply "Work hard and follow directions" may be tempting, parents and students deserve more detail. In any activity outside of school, parents would expect a clear definition of success, and they deserve the same within the school. Leaders can profitably devote the first few faculty meetings of the year to role play in which the leader assumes the role of a parent and asks this question. Teachers and leaders can collaborate in crafting the best response to the query regarding what students must know and be able to do to succeed. The time to answer that question is at the beginning of the year, not when a controversy arises about a grade or curriculum decision.

☐ **The teacher has the flexibility to vary the length and quantity of curriculum content daily to ensure that students receive more time on the most essential subjects.** This criterion is counterintuitive to many teachers and leaders, particularly if they have assumed that implementing academic standards implies standardizing teaching practice. In fact, an integral part of successful standards implementation is greater flexibility for teachers. Because student needs vary from one classroom to the next, the greatest need is flexibility in timing and emphasis, provided that this does not lead to flexibility in expectations. Therefore, administrators should devote more attention to classroom assessment and teacher expectations, not to whether each teacher is delivering the same lesson at the same time on the same day.

☐ **Students can spontaneously explain what *proficiency* means for any assignment.** Larry Lezotte asks the question well when he inquires, "What are you learning about today, and how do you know if you are learning it?" If students are unsure or hesitant, it may be time to allow them to play a greater role in restating standards and creating scoring guides. My experience suggests that if students have the opportunity to create expectations, the requirements are clearer and more rigorous than if the job of articulating requirements is left exclusively in the hands of adults.

☐ **Commonly used standards, such as those for written expression, are reinforced in every subject.** In other words, spelling, capitalization, and grammar always count. When teaching mathematics, whether to elementary students or graduate students, I begin the semester by explaining: "Mathematics is about describing the universe using numbers, symbols, and words. We will use all three this semester, and all three are important enough that we will express them correctly." Symbols, including inequalities, exponential notation, periods, and commas, are important. Words and letters, whether in an algebraic equation or an English sentence, are important. The same emphasis on clarity of expression applies to science, social studies, physical education, and music. There is, in other words, no class in any school in which English expression is unimportant or in which thinking, reasoning, and communicating are extraneous.

☐ **The teacher has created at least one standards-based performance assessment in the past month.** Training teachers in standards and standards-based assessment is not enough. The real question is whether the training is being used in the classroom. With respect to the issue of determining whether standards are really in use, the question is not whether the teacher likes standards or had a good attitude about the last training session. The only relevant question is whether an assessment the teacher creates and uses in the classroom is related to state academic standards.

☐ **The teacher exchanges student work with a colleague for review and collaborative evaluation at least once every two weeks.** Collaboration is the hallmark of effective implementation of standards. In fact, standards have never been implemented by virtue of a colorful wall chart from the state department of education. Standards have only been implemented successfully when professional educators and school leaders agree, through intensive and consistent collaborative effort, on what the word *proficient* really means.

☐ **The teacher provides feedback to students and parents about the quality of student work compared to the standards, and not compared to that of other students.** School leaders are called on to deal with this criterion when aggrieved parents notice that their child received the same score as another child, and the other child had to submit the assignment several times to be deemed proficient. "That's not fair," the parents assert. "Our child got the problem right the first time, and that child only got the problem right after working hard, respecting teacher feedback, meeting the standard, and resubmitting the work. That just can't be fair!" Leaders must support teachers in two clear rejoinders to this complaint. First, in a standards-based school, teachers never compare the work of one student to that of another student. "I'll devote an entire hour to comparing your child's work to a standard," the teacher might say, "but I will not spend a single moment comparing your child's work to that of another child. That sort of discussion is out of bounds, and I won't do it." Second, the teacher might note that, "I am quite familiar with the academic standards of this state, and not a single one of them requires that our students complete proficiency quickly. In fact, not a single standard refers to speed, but all of them refer to the quality of work. Therefore, I evaluate student work on the basis of the standards and the quality of work, never in comparison of one student to another."

☐ **The teacher helps to build community consensus in the classroom and with other stakeholders for standards and high expectations of all students.** National polling data make clear that the teacher is a trusted purveyor of information, particularly about educational policy. Voters trust teachers more than they trust board members, state policy makers, or school administrators. Therefore, teachers bear particular responsibility for carrying the message of the fairness and effectiveness of academic standards. Effective leaders give teachers the tools, time, and opportunity to practice effective communication with the community at large. Role-playing dialogue with skeptical community stakeholders is an excellent practice for a faculty meeting or professional development seminar.

☐ **The teacher uses a variety of assessment techniques, including extended written response, in all disciplines.**

A.17. School Checklist for Standards Implementation

☐ Faculty meetings are routinely devoted to collaborative examination of real student work compared to academic standards.

☐ There are schoolwide assessments administered to every student in the same class (secondary) or grade (elementary) at periodic intervals.

☐ Professional development is based on an analysis of teacher familiarity with and application of essential skills in standards-based instruction (see checklist A-22).

☐ Student performance in key standards is posted monthly or quarterly, with the "percentage proficient or higher" tracked during the year.

☐ Eighty percent or more of the faculty agree on the standards-based scoring of an anonymous piece of student work.

☐ The principal personally participates in evaluating student work at least once a week.

☐ Students who do not meet academic standards receive immediate and decisive intervention, including mandatory tutoring and schedule adjustments.

☐ A review of the agenda and minutes of faculty meetings, grade-level meetings, and department meetings reveals an overwhelming focus (90 percent or more of agenda items and time) on academic achievement and collaborative scoring of student work.

☐ Faculty meetings are held jointly with other schools at least once a quarter to ensure that there are comparable expectations for student achievement.

☐ Teachers evaluate student achievement on the basis of performance compared to standards and not on the normal curve, any comparison to other students, or average performance during the grading period.

☐ The grading reporting system allows teachers to give a narrative explanation for student work, including an alternative explanation for letter grades.

☐ Analysis of data—including test data, classroom assessments, and professional practices in teaching, curriculum, and leadership—are regularly reviewed. The building leader can readily articulate specific changes made since the previous semester that are directly related to this data analysis.

☐ The building leadership regularly identifies best practices, documenting in detail successful practice in teaching, curriculum, and leadership, and sharing it with all faculty members.

☐ The building leadership conducts a "weed the garden" exercise at least once a semester and can identify initiatives and activities that have been dropped in the past six months.

☐ The school analyzes data at the level of classroom and building to analyze the relationship between teaching, curriculum, and leadership indicators and student results. These results are analyzed on the Leadership and Learning Matrix; the most effective practices are shared with all faculty members.

☐ School goals are obvious, regularly measured, and understood by faculty and students. List school goals here and note evidence of regular measurement:

A.18. District Checklist for Standards Implementation

☐ The district curriculum clearly reflects state academic content standards and adds value to those standards through prioritization and focus.

☐ The district has gathered consensus from every building on the standards for each grade that are essential for the next level of instruction. The consensus power standards have been shared throughout the district.

☐ The district regularly identifies and shares best practices in standards-based teaching, assessment, and curriculum.

☐ The district regularly conducts a weed-the-garden exercise and can identify specific initiatives and activities that have been dropped in the past six months.

☐ The district monitors information requests and other requirements from the central office to classrooms and buildings and reports to the superintendent monthly the nature of those information requests and other requirements and their relationship to student achievement.

☐ The district accountability plan includes not only test scores but also building and classroom-based practices in teaching, curriculum, and leadership.

☐ The district regularly identifies the relationship between effective practice and student results using the Leadership and Learning Matrix.

☐ The board has established standards for its own conduct, including standards regarding communication with faculty members and information requests from buildings, classrooms, and central office departments.

Appendix B
Leadership Discipline in Action: Linking Your Time with Your Mission

B.1. Time Log

Instructions: Maintain a detailed log of time for two weeks. Use categories that are appropriate for you. Examples of categories to enter in the columns: planning, e-mail and voice mail responses, exercise, professional reading, counseling direct reports, staff meetings, parent meetings, student contact, community meetings, travel, community service, and family.

Date: _____

[Enter your categories for each column.]

From (start time)	To (end time)	Total time (fraction of 1 hour)	Category

Total: _____

Today's total hours: _____

After collecting at least fourteen of these daily records, construct a pie chart that reflects your actual time allocation. Compare it to your priorities, and evaluate whether changes are appropriate in how you allocate your most important resource: your time.

B.2. Leadership Journal

Keep a journal with the most important questions that force you to address your key challenges. After you have accumulated entries for several weeks, discuss them with a mentor, coach, colleague, or other trusted person.

Date: _____

- What did you learn today?
- Whom did you nurture today?
- What difficult issue did you confront today?
- What is your most important challenge right now?
- What did you do today to make progress on your most important challenge?

Other questions that address your central challenges:

B.3. Master Task List

Instructions: Use this form to start your time management system. Using as many pages as you need, list every task that is now pending for you. Because you are using a single comprehensive system, include all tasks related to family obligations, professional requirements, community service, and others from any list that you keep. The start of your journey to effective time management is the use of a single list for all tasks. Prioritize each task using these codes:

A = Must be done by you and only you

B = Should be done by you, but will give way to A-level tasks

C = Request to be done by you, but can be delayed or delegated to others

Name: _____

Date: _____

Page ____ of ____ pages

Task	Priority (A, B, C)	Date Originated

B.4. Daily Prioritized Task List

Note: Create a new prioritized task list every day. Throughout the day, add to it any new requests for your time. If you have more than six A priorities for today, then you must either defer some of the A-level tasks or change some to B-level priority.

Name: _____

Date: _____

Page _____ of _____ pages

Task	Priority (A, B, C)	Date Originated

B.5. Project Task List

Instructions: Projects must be broken down into manageable tasks. Any task that takes more than the time allowed for a single uninterrupted work session must be broken down into several tasks. In general, if a task takes more than three hours to complete, it is not a task but a project.

Project name: _____

Start date: _____

Task	Person Responsible	Start Date	Deadline

Appendix C
The Daily Disciplines
of Leadership Worksheet

1. Define objectives on the basis of the mission.

2. Create standards of action; what must the organization do?

3. Develop an assessment tool. How will you know if you are successful? How will you know if you are exemplary? How will you know if you have not yet achieved success?

4. Implement an accountability system. Measure both organizational results and the specific actions (of individuals and of the organization) that are intended to produce those results.

5. Provide continuous feedback. Analyze the relationship (or lack of relationship) between action and results, and refocus organizational energy and resources on the strategies that are most closely related to desired results.

Date: _____

Write down the objectives you are working on *today*:

If you are to achieve those objectives, what must the organization do? These are objective standards of action. In answer to the question, "Did you meet the standard of action?" you can receive a *yes* or *no* response.

Standards of action:	

Assessment:	Describe each level of performance.
	Exemplary:
	Proficient:
	Approaching proficiency:
	Not meeting standard:

Accountability:	What are the "dashboard" indicators you can track every day that are most important in achieving your objectives and mission?
Indicators:	

Feedback:	How will the information you gather change your decisions?

Write one example of how you used feedback to change your allocation of resources or time, or otherwise improved your decision making:

Appendix D
Leadership Focus Worksheet:
The Obstacles Between
Knowing and Doing

We Know	We Must Do:	Obstacles Between Knowing and Doing	How I Will Deal with the Obstacle (Change the obstacle, go around it, or remove it)

Appendix E
Stakeholder Participation Matrix

Directions: In the left-hand column, list all the stakeholder groups that you can think of for your community. They might include students, parents, the taxpayers association, teachers union, administrators' association, and other stakeholders relevant to your community. Across the column headings, list the major influence groups that regularly bring matters to the board. They might include the accountability task force, the strategic planning committee, the community relations committee, and other groups that interface with the board and community. Write the number of stakeholder groups represented for each column. If there is no representation, leave that box blank. Use this tool to identify which groups are most and least represented in communication with the board.

Stakeholders						

Appendix F
Leadership Standards Development

Instructions: Use this form to create standards and identify performance evidence for each leadership criterion. Your organization will probably have several leadership criteria, such as integrity, supervision, planning, and communication, to name a few. For each criterion, use a separate form. In the left-hand column, identify the standards that describe in specific detail your expectations for the leader. In the right-hand column, write the evidence that you will collect for each standard.

Leadership criterion: _____

Standards	Evidence

References

Ackerman, R. H., Donaldson, G. A., and Van Der Bogert, R. *Making Sense as a School Leader: Persisting Questions, Creative Opportunities*. San Francisco: Jossey-Bass, 1996.

Anderson, G. "Achieving Excellence and Equity in Education: An Integrated Approach to Improving Student Achievement." Houston: APQC Education Initiative, 2001.

Barth, R. S. *Improving Schools from Within: Teacher, Parents, and Principals Can Make the Difference*. San Francisco: Jossey-Bass, 1990.

Benfari, R. C. *Understanding and Changing Your Management Style*. San Francisco: Jossey-Bass, 1999.

Bennis, W. *Old Dogs, New Tricks*. Provo, Utah: Executive Excellence, 1999.

Boyatzis, R., McKee, A., and Goleman, D. "Reawakening Your Passion for Work." *Harvard Business Review*, Apr. 2002, pp. 87–94.

Buckingham, M., and Coffman, C. *First, Break All the Rules: What the World's Greatest Managers Do Differently*. New York: Simon & Schuster, 1999.

Calkins, L. *The Art of Teaching Writing* (new ed.). Portsmouth, N.H.: Heinemann, 1994.

Cambridge Group. (Review of *Strategics: The Art and Science of Holistic Strategy*, by W. J. Cook, Jr.) Montgomery, Ala.: Cambridge Group. 2002. (www.colonialcambridge.com/product.html)

Ciampa, D., and Watkins, M. *Right from the Start: Taking Charge in a New Leadership Role*. Boston: Harvard Business School Press, 1999.

Collins, J. *Good to Great: Why Some Companies Make the Leap . . . and Others Don't*. New York: HarperBusiness, 2001.

Collins, J. C., and Porras, J. I. *Built to Last: Successful Habits of Visionary Companies*. New York: HarperBusiness, 1994.

Darling-Hammond, L. *The Right to Learn: A Blueprint for Creating Schools That Work*. San Francisco: Jossey-Bass, 1997.

De Pree, M. *Leadership Jazz*. New York: Doubleday, 1992.

Drucker, P. F. *Management Challenges for the 21st Century*. New York: HarperBusiness, 1999.

Epstein, M. J., and Birchard, B. *Counting What Counts: Turning Corporate Accountability to Competitive Advantage.* Reading, Mass.: Perseus, 1999.

Fullan, M., and Hargreaves, A. *What's Worth Fighting for in Your School?* New York: Teachers College Press, 1996.

Gardner, H. *The Disciplined Mind: What All Students Should Understand.* New York: Simon & Schuster, 1999.

Gary, L. "Fostering Change While Avoiding the Road to Martyrdom." *Harvard Management Update,* 2002, 7(4), 7–8.

Goleman, D. *Working with Emotional Intelligence.* New York: Bantam, 1998.

Goleman, D. *Primal Leadership.* Boston: Harvard Business School Press, 2002.

Goodlad, J. I. *Educational Renewal: Better Teachers, Better Schools.* San Francisco: Jossey-Bass, 1994.

Gullatt, D. E., and Ritter, M. L. "What Is Your Grade? Researchers Look at How States Determine the Effectiveness of Schools." *American School Board Journal,* 2002, 189(2), 40–42.

Hamel, G. *Leading the Revolution.* Boston: Harvard Business School Press, 2000.

Hammer, M. *The Agenda: What Every Business Must Do to Dominate the Decade.* New York: Crown Business, 2001.

Hargrove, R. *Mastering the Art of Creative Collaboration.* New York: McGraw-Hill, 1998.

Haycock, K. "Good Teaching Matters: How Well-Qualified Teachers Can Close the Gap." *Thinking K-16,* Summer 1998.

Haycock, K. "*Dispelling the Myth* Revisited." 2002. (www.edtrust.org)

Haycock, K., and others (eds.). *Dispelling the Myth: High Poverty Schools Exceeding Expectations.* Washington, D.C.: Education Trust, 1999.

Hersey, P. *Situational Leader.* New York: Warner, 1992.

Hersey, P., and Blanchard, K. *Management of Organizational Behavior: Utilizing Human Resources* (6th ed.). Upper Saddle River, N.J.: Prentice Hall, 1993.

Holloway, L. "Increasingly, the Principal Is a Newcomer." New York Times, Oct. 2, 2001. (http://query.nytimes.com/search/restricted/articles= FB0A15F939590C718CDDA90994D9404482)

Internet Nonprofit Center. 2002. (www.nonprofits.org)

Kaplan, R. S., and Norton, D. P. *The Balanced Scorecard: Translating Strategy into Action.* Boston: Harvard Business School Press, 1996.

Kaplan, R. S., and Norton, D. P. *The Strategy-Focused Organization: How Balanced Scorecard Companies Thrive in the New Business Environment.* Boston: Harvard Business School Press, 2001.

King, M. L., Jr. (Quotation in Chapter Five.) Columbia World of Quotations, 1996. (www.bartleby.com/66/97/32697.html)

Klentschy, M., Garrison, L., and Amaral, O. M. "Valle Imperiale Project in Science (VIPS)" (National Science Foundation grant no. ESI-9731274), 2000.

Kotter, J. P. *Leading Change: An Action Plan from the World's Foremost Expert on Business Leadership.* Boston: Harvard Business School Press, 1996.

Kotter, J. P. *On What Leaders Really Do*. Boston: Harvard Business School Press, 1999.

Kotter, J. P. *The Heart of Change*. Boston: Harvard Business School Press, 2002. Quoted in "Something They Can Take to Heart: The Power of See-Feel-Change." *Harvard Management Update*, 2002, 7(4), 3.

Levitt, T. *Thinking About Management*. New York: Free Press, 1991.

Parson, M. J. *An Executive's Coaching Handbook Action Dialogue for the Fair, Effective and Appropriate Management of Individuals and Staffs*. New York: Facts on File, 1986.

Peters, T., and Austin, N. *A Passion for Excellence: The Leadership Difference*. New York: Random House, 1985.

Peters, T. J., and Waterman, R. H., Jr. *In Search of Excellence: Lessons from America's Best-Run Companies*. New York: Random House, 1982.

Pfeffer, J. *The Human Equation: Building Profits by Putting People First*. Boston: Harvard Business School Press, 1998.

RAND Corporation. "Implementation and Performance in New American Schools: Three Years into Scale-Up." 2001. (www.rand.org/publications/MR/MR1145)

Reeves, D. B. *Accountability in Action: A Blueprint for Learning Organizations*. Denver: Advanced Learning Press, 2000a.

Reeves, D. B. "Accountability for Student Learning." (Video Journal of Education, vol. 1001.) Salt Lake City: Linton Professional Development, 2000b.

Reeves D. B. "Standards Are Not Enough: Essential Transformations for Successful Schools." *NASSP Bulletin*, 2000c, 84(610), 5–19.

Reeves, D. B. *Crusade in the Classroom: How George W. Bush's Education Reforms Will Affect Your Children, Our Schools*. New York: Simon & Schuster, 2001a.

Reeves, D. B. "Essential Transformations for Successful Schools." Presentation to the National Standards Conference, Las Vegas, Apr. 4, 2001b.

Reeves, D. B. "Galileo's Dilemma: Scientific Research in Education." *Education Week*, 2002a, 21(34), pp. 44, 33.

Reeves, D. B. *Holistic Accountability: Serving Students, Schools, and Community*. Thousand Oaks, Calif.: Corwin, 2002b.

Reeves, D. B. *Making Standards Work: How to Implement Standards-Based Performance Assessments in the Classroom, School, and District* (3rd ed.). Denver: Advanced Learning Press, 2002c.

Sack, J. "Experts Debate Effect of Whole School Reform." *Education Week*, Jan. 30, 2002, p. 6.

Schmoker, M. *The Results Fieldbook: Practical Strategies from Dramatically Improved Schools*. Alexandria, Va.: Association for Supervision and Curriculum Development, 2001.

Senge, P. *The Fifth Discipline: The Art and Practice of the Learning Organization*. New York: Doubleday, 1990.

Sergiovanni, T. *The Lifeworld of Leadership: Creating Culture, Community, and Personal Meaning in Our Schools*. San Francisco: Jossey-Bass, 2000.

Shtogren, J. A. (ed.) *Skyhooks for Leadership: A New Framework That Brings Together Five Decades of Thought—from Maslow to Senge*. New York: AMACOM, 1999.

Stricherz, M. "Groups Pushing for Measures to Attract, Retain Principals." *Education Week*, July 11, 2001. (www.edweek.org/ew/ewstory.cfm?slug=42principals.h20&keywords=Principal%20Shortage)

Tichy, N. M. *The Leadership Engine: How Winning Companies Build Leaders at Every Level*. New York: HarperCollins, 1997.

Ulrich, D., Zenger, J., and Smallwood, N. *Results-Based Leadership: How Leaders Build the Business and Improve the Bottom Line*. Boston: Harvard Business School Press, 1999.

Useem, M. *The Leadership Moment: Nine True Stories of Triumph and Disaster and Their Lessons for Us All*. New York: Random House, 1998.

Viadero, D. "Whole School Projects Show Mixed Results." *Education Week*, Nov. 7, 2001, pp. 1ff.

Vicere, A. A., and Fulmer, R. M. *Leadership by Design: How Benchmark Companies Sustain Success Through Investment in Continuous Learning*. Boston: Harvard Business School Press, 1997.

Wheatley, M. J. *Leadership and the New Science: Discovering Order in a Chaotic World*. San Francisco: Berrett-Koehler, 1999.

Index